FAR FROM DENMARK

FAR FROM DENMARK

Peter Martins

WITH ROBERT CORNFIELD

LITTLE, BROWN AND COMPANY   BOSTON / TORONTO

FIRST EDITION

Title page photograph © *William Christensen*

LIBRARY OF CONGRESS CATALOGING IN PUBLICATION DATA

Martins, Peter.
  Far from Denmark.

  Includes index.
  1. Martins, Peter. 2. Ballet dancers — Denmark —
Biography. 3. New York City Ballet. I. Cornfield,
Robert. II. Title.
GV1785.M34A34   1982   792.8′2′0924 [B]   82-14906
ISBN 0-316-54855-3

MU
Designed by Susan Windheim

Published simultaneously in Canada
by Little, Brown & Company (Canada) Limited

PRINTED IN THE UNITED STATES OF AMERICA

for my mother
and Stanley Williams

With my son, Nilas, some years ago (© William Christensen)

INTRODUCTION

by Robert Cornfield

This book is a dancer's and choreographer's description of his craft — that of dancing and making dances. In recent years Peter Martins has demonstrated his proficiency as a choreographer, and on the basis of the dozen or so ballets he has made, we know already that his will be a significant contribution to the ballet repertoire. His works are in the repertory of the New York City Ballet where he has been a principal dancer since 1970, and where he serves, since the fall of 1981, as a ballet master, joining in that capacity George Balanchine, Jerome Robbins and John Taras. His position is sufficient claim for him to be considered a major figure in dance in the United States.

What is also becoming clearer about Peter Martins is the imprint his dancing has made. His influence is not as easy to delineate as is his choreographic achievement. Dancing can be written about and filmed, and steps can be noted, but how dancers provide examples and extend the range of their craft — technically, emotionally, expressively, ideationally — is not so easily shown. Nonetheless, Peter Martins has altered the course of male dancing in America. The full impact of his example will be clearer as the years go by, when his contributions will also include that of company director and teacher in addition to dancer and choreographer. There is good reason to begin now to take the measure of this extraordinary dance artist.

It is convenient and truthful to begin a description of a dancer with a national tag; and with justice we can say, for instance, that Anthony

Dowell exemplifies and provides a model for English classical dance. Peter Martins writes that Suzanne Farrell and Edward Villella are the supreme examples of American dancing (classical, for this book is about ballet), and we can continue the game with examples of Russians — Vyacheslav Gordeyev and Vladimir Vasiliev — with a category of International Russian for the most celebrated dancers of our time, Rudolph Nureyev, Natalia Makarova, and Mikhail Baryshnikov.

These dancers embody a national character we recognize and the way they dance classical ballet is nationally inflected. They give their dancing a distinct accent by stressing certain facilities (jumps, turns, speed) over others; and by acting in a manner we know as Russian, or American. There are only four dance styles that are consequential: the English, American, Russian and Danish. I can think of no other country that at present offers the kind of distinctions these do, though other countries have celebrated dance companies.

Peter Martins is a Danish dancer. How then has he managed to influence American style? To answer this we have to outline a social history of male dancing in America.

At the time Peter Martins arrived in this country, American male dancers were proposing a new answer to the question: What was a clean-cut American boy doing on stage in tights? In the thirties, a number of American dancers disguised themselves as Russians to receive credibility as classical dancers* (a situation satirized in the Fred Astaire movie *Shall We Dance* — the Great Petrov is really Peter P. Peters) and probably they not only assumed Russianized names but manners as well. We know though from the careers of the Christensen brothers and others that by their talent and achievement some Americans had won the right to be named outstanding classical dancers. In the forties and fifties another answer was found and that was a hearty, bright-boy manner that seemed closer to the characteristics of musical comedy dancing. A too-often-told tale is the story of ballet's

---

*The American Marcel Le Plat joined De Basil's Ballet Russe as Marc Platoff, and changed his name to Marc Platt when he joined the cast of *Oklahoma*.

influence on show choreography — as a sideline, Balanchine, Agnes de Mille, and Robbins remade the genre — but we can tell the tale of Broadway coming to Ballet through the brash stage presence of some dancers.

In the late fifties and through the sixties a new approach emerged, an additional response to the question, and that was that dancers were athletes in makeup, and tights were really a variety of gym attire. Not that American dancers hadn't always been strong, but now came an insistence that ballet was as tough as football, as fast as basketball, as elegant as tennis. It was a world of macho tough-guys. The consequence was that dancers worried about strength, stamina, and a developed physique to the detriment of perfect placement and line and accurate performance of the classical vocabulary: they needed something more aggressively masculine. What with the overlay of good-guy mannerisms derived from popular and show dancing, we had good-guy macho athletes as Albrecht and Siegfried.

The force of American classical dancers like Jacques d'Amboise and Edward Villella had some origin in a certain defensiveness, and that battle to insist on the "maleness" of a dancer worked to the benefit of the art. It urged a new definition and indeed fostered a new way of dancing that is a vital part of the American style. That classical ballet could absorb athleticism was a euphoric discovery.

These rough-and-ready dance mannerisms were what Peter Martins found here and says he couldn't understand — for such artistic insecurities were not part of his background or education. He had early on learned the pride of dancing, and that pride is now instinctive in him. (Also, he believes that dancing well is a moral imperative for those who have the talent. That belief is his most severely held.) I think that he understood this dilemma of the American dancer and he understood the solution perfectly — what he had to find was his place in this scheme.

He felt American dancing was needlessly smothered in personality and drama, while his intention has always been to leave his dancing uncluttered, to strip it down, to make it, not impersonal, but lucid. (This doesn't preclude characterization or mime, or delineating a work's special atmosphere, for he is a great actor.) His solution to becoming an American dancer was a remarkable one: he did not modify his identity as a dancer — he maintained his technical and moral approach — and showed that this purity, devoid of ruggedness, could serve to produce as vivid an "American" effect. Peter Martins proved that he could be a Balanchine dancer and he could be himself. There was no conflict, or if there was he illustrated how it could be resolved, for he knew how to stretch his manner and technique, without the loss of any integrity.

He demonstrated that elegance, refinement, assured, unobtrusive partnering, clarity and delicacy could be masculine distinctions. His dancing in American neoclassical works shone with the clarity of classical ballet. His tact and stance showed that American dancing could include all these and still be vigorous and energetic and alert. He found how to dance "Balanchine" within the dictates of that approach's own terms, and on his own terms. Today, the young dancers in the New York City Ballet imitate him — much of what they have learned about dancing has come by watching him.

A major element of his distinction has been his adaptive ability, for no other "import" managed to the degree he did such an adaptation. Why? I suspect it has to do with his dance intelligence and his intellectual breadth — this intelligence enables him to be immediately sympathetic to all styles, to "get them," and to make them part of his own dancing. But it wasn't this remarkable facility for encompassing other styles that accounts for his importance to young American dancers.

In Denmark his primary teacher was Stanley Williams, who came to the United States some few years before Peter Martins did to teach at the School of American Ballet. Stanley Williams has trained over a generation of dancers here and he has overseen Peter Martins's American career.

The impact of George Balanchine and New York reshaped Peter Martins, but when asked how he had changed over the years, he answered, "You know, I'm exactly the way I've always been. Maybe my ideas have changed but essentially I'm the same." What George Balanchine and New

York did was help Peter Martins to realize himself, and without the example and direction of George Balanchine Peter Martins would not be the man we know.

Peter Martins has steered clear of being a superstar, and lists the desire for fame and success as a pitfall for dancers, something they must be on their guard against. There is no other reason to dance but the joy of doing it, and maybe that contact with the sublime. His most realistic evaluation is just this: if you have the gift to be an artist, then you must be that. It's worth everything. Its reward is itself.

His dancing is not so much Olympian as Platonic — he is concerned with the idea of dancing, with the beauty of the dance forms. The weight of his emotional involvement is his sensitivity to shape — and because of this he seems distant, grand, composed. He serves this craft, and he purposefully divests himself so that dancing for dancing's sake is the clearest message. He presents us with dancing: he shows the splendor of its matter. Probably better than any other dancer he makes us *see* classical dancing. He trusts his personality and his physicality so completely that he doesn't have to promote them. The relaxation of the issues of personality and meaning and extraneous matter is probably what George Balanchine and Peter Martins recognized in each other. As this book shows, the master and disciple were in agreement before they met.

The fullest expression of his personality is his choreography. Part of the joyful relief of that work for him, why he is such an eager choreographer, is that he has found "self-expression." I see Peter Martins's wit in his *Calcium Light Night*, the precision of his thought in *Sonate di Scarlatti*, his romantic imagination in *Tchaikovsky Symphony No. 1*, his prankishness and sentimentality in *The Magic Flute*, and his caustic limning of relationships in *L'Histoire du Soldat*. Peter Martins has kept nothing back from dance; he has given all of himself to it.

Our work together on this book began with conversations, and from our notes and memory of those talks we produced a first draft which we revised and then rewrote together, and then revised once again. Our intention was a book about dancing from a dancer's perspective, with Peter using his experiences as the instances.

We are very grateful to our friends whose best advice we probably haven't heeded, but where we have accepted help the book is the better for it. We'd like to thank especially Deborah Koolish, Robert Gottlieb, Nilas Martins, Leslie Bailey, and our patient but firm editor, Genevieve Young.

CONTENTS

CHAPTER ONE

Learning to Dance

Each year, in June, at the end of the Royal Theatre season in Copenhagen, auditions are held for the ballet school. Children, for the most part between the ages of eight and eleven, come to the school for the entrance examination. The audition room is an old ballet studio with worn wooden floors whose walls are lined with portraits of August Bournonville, and in one corner is a bust of this nineteenth-century ballet master and choreographer who created the Danish ballet style.

In small groups the children are seated in a row and asked to remove their shoes. The ballet master and some teachers walk slowly down the line, the ballet master sometimes holding a baton. The children raise their feet, and the shape and extent of each arch is scrutinized, the curve of the instep examined. The foot is a clue to potential ability — the children are being examined for a crucial indication of a dancer's physical equipment. When I was a child, in the early fifties, what was wanted at the Royal Danish Ballet School was a small foot with a big arch and a big instep.

Next, the children are asked to stand and their overall proportions are considered. No low legs (short limbs), no extra-long legs. The teachers are looking for a pleasing appearance, and for the perfectly proportioned. But talent can override all shortcomings (in my case it had to override big feet).

The next test is a dance, and the dance is a simple waltz. The students are arranged in a circle, and since most of them have had classes in social dancing the test is an easy one, but it demonstrates grace and musicality and how the body moves. Intelligence isn't being tested, but it will be demanded later on.

Equipment, proportion, musicality, and intelligence: these make a dancer. (Well, and talent and dedication.)

In a country whose total population is five million, approximately fifty children are accepted, and the school's total enrollment is two hundred and fifty. Of these only a few finish out the course, for each year the students are tested, and the unpromising weeded out. A very select number of those who graduate are asked to join the Royal Danish Ballet.

It was in 1954, when I was eight, that I was accepted in the school.

My mother's side of the family was entirely involved with music or dance, and my mother, a pianist, traces this predilection to her own mother who, unknown to her parents, spent many childhood days with the local Copenhagen circus, entertaining between acts, doing small errands, learning simple acrobatic feats. Her thwarted theatrical ambitions blossomed in her children. My mother's brother, Leif Ornberg, had been a leading dancer with the Royal Danish Ballet before the war and his wife had been a prima ballerina. An uncle was a percussionist in the Theatre Orchestra, and a cousin who was in the ballet company was married to a violinist. Another aunt had her own dance academy. Ours was a family steeped in the arts, and my mother saw no reason why her son shouldn't continue the tradition.

My father, an engineer whose designs and ambitions for a native-made Danish automobile came to nothing because of the industry halt caused by the war, seemingly had no interest in dance, or in any of the arts for that matter. He and my mother were divorced when I was two, and he never exerted any influence on my choice of a career.

As it happened, my heritage and family connections were of no help to me when I first attended the Royal Danish Ballet School. In retrospect, they seem to have created problems. My sisters Marianne and Annette auditioned the same day I did and were not accepted for reasons that are still unclear. Some of my relatives felt there were teachers and dancers who intensely disliked my family for political reasons stemming from the war, that we children were being victimized for quarrels that had nothing to do with us. It's likely that my acceptance was based on their being short of boys, a problem shared by dance schools all over the world.

At the end of each school year, for seven straight years, my mother received a letter from the school authorities: "Peter is possibly talented, maybe he has some aptitude, perhaps some gift, but we have not made a conclusive decision, and we must warn you that we are still watching his progress. So we leave you with the caution that this next year might be his last at the school."

The school is a full scholarship school, and all my expenses, including

4

dance shoes and class clothes, were covered. Ballet classes were held in the morning; in the afternoon we had our academic subjects, and at the end of the school day were rehearsals for performances, for the theater seasons were a mix of ballet, opera and drama, all of which used children to fill out the stage picture.

After the divorce, my mother had moved with my sisters and me to a small apartment. Being the sole male, I had a room to myself, while my sisters shared one. The forty-five-minute trip to school involved two street-cars, and when the weather was good (it rains a lot in Copenhagen) I'd cycle. For lunch, my mother packed open-faced sandwiches of salami, liver pâté, thin slabs of chocolate, banana on dark pumpernickel. I would exchange the chocolate and banana with an agreeable schoolmate for more liver pâté.

After school I would go home for an early supper, return to the theater to perform, and then go back home by myself after the performance. Copenhagen was a safe city, and I wasn't afraid of traveling alone; besides, I was armed with the privilege of being a student at the school, a paid performer, of being among the Elect.

My first years at the school were not pleasant for me — I didn't feel liked by the staff and instructors and I sensed a personal antipathy because of my family. But even at that age, I had enormous pride and would have thought it an unendurable disgrace and, even more, a family dishonor if I had been expelled. No matter how much I loathed the school, I felt I had no choice but to remain, and to excel. This effort forged a quality that turned out to be a strength in later years: a faith in my talent, an assurance that was developed not by constant praise from others but from an inner, self-sustained belief in myself.

From the age of five I had social dance classes, and I always felt good at it. For five straight years, my partner and I won the silver medal in the Danish National Social Dancing Competition, losing out to the same couple every year for the gold medal (the contest consisted of dancing a waltz, tango, quick step, paso-doble, fox-trot, rumba). The winning boy was the son of Denmark's leading social dance teacher, and in the sixth year I finally beat him. With that accomplished, I retired from social dancing competitions. Dancing was something I did better than any of my classmates. It was easy (then), and I just did it. I realized afterward that I didn't have to search out an ambition. I'd be a dancer and that was fine. I don't remember being tempted by anything else, except for brief teenage fantasies of seeing myself as a canny, swell-suited lawyer or powerful, gritty, tough soccer player. Dancing suited me.

What I remember is that in my early teens I was a rowdy, quarrelsome, snotty kid, completely undisciplined, known as an instigator and a troublemaker. I fought most often with another hell-raiser, and another Peter, the son of Frank Schaufuss, the company's director. Some people thought I was pampered at home because I was the only male, but that was hardly the case. If anything, my sisters and my mother made a point of not spoiling me, and to my way of looking at things, they gave me a rough time to keep me from thinking I was anything special. My complaint would have been that I was *too* disciplined — I had all the chores, except for washing the dishes (my sisters did that). But my rebellion was not at home, it was at school.

Stanley Williams, who was a principal dancer with the company and who was also on the teaching staff, became my teacher when I was twelve. He had been born in England but his mother was Danish and his family moved to Denmark when he was a child. Stanley Williams is my teacher. When a dancer says, "So-and-So is my teacher," he means this is the one who determined my style, who gave me the clue to the art and to my way of performing. This is the teacher who set my goals, who set my standards of movement. It was Stanley Williams who made me feel the challenge, the potential achievement, the *importance* of being a dancer.

In Stanley's class I was well behaved. I worked hard, trying to gain his attention and his respect. He became that figure of authority, that guide and model who gives shape and purpose to a boy's ambition, who embodies a young man's image of who he wants to be, who he wants to be like. (I hold only one tiny little thing against Stanley to this day, and that is his

My uncle, Leif Ornberg

My aunt, Elna Lauesgaard

With my sisters, Annette and Marianne

With my aunt Rudi

With my mother and sisters

My days as a champion social dancer

At the Royal Danish Ballet School, (opposite page) being taught by Hans Brenaa beneath a bust of Bournonville; (below) in front of the Royal Danish Theatre with a friend

callousness in making me break in his nasty little ballet shoes in class — supposedly this was an honor — for his performances when my own huge feet should have been developing in their own free way, wearing their own shoes.)

Years later, I heard how tenuous my position at the school really had been, of how Stanley maneuvered to keep me from being thrown out. The first year I took class with Stanley I was still taking class with another teacher, a teacher I had little respect for, and I was very concerned with doing everything the way Stanley taught.

The problem came to a head on one specific issue. The other teacher insisted that at the barre during the *tendu* exercises (stretching the legs to the front, side and back) I keep my free arm out to the side throughout, whereas Stanley taught more of an active *port de bras*, moving the arm to the front on occasion. I became irritated when the teacher constantly corrected what I had been taught by Stanley and in one class I pointedly held my arm out to the side between barre exercises, while the teacher was explaining what we were to do next. My behavior was considered to be provocative and contemptuous, and I was thrown out of the class immediately.

The director of the school gave me a letter to take to my mother. She never told me what it said but I remained at home, in terror, for the next few days.

Then there was a meeting between the teacher and Stanley before the director at which the teacher threatened to resign if I weren't expelled. Stanley thought it absurd to be making such a fuss over a bad-mannered twelve-year-old, and besides, he said, the kid had some promise. You don't kick out talented youngsters because they are brats. You shape them up. Throwing kids out because of this kind of action was no way to run a school.

Unrelenting, the teacher persisted, insisting that I was stupid and obstinate. This wasn't the first instance of my rudeness and disrespect. I must go, or he would. Stanley was shocked at this tirade, which seemed to

him about as immature as my behavior, and his only choice was to coun-
terattack, insisting that if I were dismissed, he'd leave with me. He hated
this business of threats, but if they were going to be flung around, here
was his.

My punishment was suspension. Stanley's argument had won out. The
director told the other teacher I was a student who must be dealt with and
controlled, not thrown out the window. There was another result of this
quarrel: Stanley had made a strong enemy, and the carping complaints about
his methods would grow in intensity.

It was Stanley's example that held me to the school through my
adolescent rebellion: cutting morning classes by claiming the streetcar was
late, or calling in sick and wandering about the city. I fancied myself an all-
around tough-guy: smoking in the halls, ripping off T-shirts from the
department store opposite the school.

Stanley was the first person I met who gave the impression that what
he did, dance and teach, was of major importance; that mastering the art
of dance is not easy but that to do so is a thunderous, almost miraculous,
achievement.

Specifically, he taught me the importance of precision, of doing steps
correctly, fully, so that each move is clear and accurate — the feet in first,
second, fifth positions absolutely clear — no muddy approximations, no
fuzziness — dancing in control, in shape, concentrating on proper form.
Dance with responsibility to the steps. You couldn't just go out there and
fly around and be extreme and dramatic, jump high and turn and turn. You
had to know *how* to turn, how to land, how to present yourself, how to
carry yourself, and you had to feel the relationship of one step to the other
within the musical phrase. It always had to be pleasing to the eye, and never
show strain; you did the most up to the point that strain entered.

He emphasized turnout — the opening out of the legs, showing to
the front as full an image of the body as possible. He concentrated on
turning, the body shown all round, revolving around an announced center

within. He demanded that the linking of steps, moving from position to position, have energy and point. The stress was on correctness and quality, not on extravagant virtuosity.

The world of Danish ballet was an insular one, and I knew little, if anything, about the world of dance beyond. What I had were books, with pictures of dancers, and I felt no relationship to these foreigners, although I was filled with curiosity. There were two dancers whose photographic images fascinated me, and these images fixed themselves in my mind. One was of Alicia Alonso. I had never seen anyone so beautiful, even just in photograph so vividly alive, and the other was of the English dancer John Gilpin.

Alonso was the first dancer who seemed to me to be the personification of female beauty, and Gilpin had an unmistakable presence, a forceful bearing that allowed me to imagine exactly what his dancing must have been like. They shared one thing in common: they looked like splendid sculptures. And if there wasn't a picture of either of them in the ballet book I was browsing through in a bookstore, then I wouldn't bother nabbing it. (I had another crush, but not on a dancer. It was on Debbie Reynolds, most especially in *Tammy*. I must have seen it eighteen times and I had a forty-five record of the title song and would lock the door to my bedroom and play it over and over, singing along. I wrote her twice. She never answered.) The movies started my romance with America, and I thought that the landscapes of Westerns and the streets of New York were where I'd be most at home. The way people in American movies behaved seemed open and free and perfect, just the right way to be. What I felt about America was that it was huge and open and busy. And I was like that. Copenhagen, I could see, was a little place — and I suddenly saw it, from what I learned from the movies, as confining — while this movie America was big, full of energy.

The style of the Royal Danish Ballet, though there had been attempts to expand it, was insular as well, and its essentials had been determined by

August Bournonville in the nineteenth century. In my third year at the school I began learning Bournonville technique. Each day (Monday through Saturday) I took a "Bournonville class," a different class for each day of the week. The class would open with the same exercises: *adagio*, *port de bras*, *tendu*, *pirouette*; but there would be a different set of variations and lengthy series of steps set to music (*enchaînements*) from Bournonville ballets or created by him as class exercises. These daily classes had been arranged by Bournonville's disciples after his death so that his methods and techniques would not be lost. These classes have been handed down from generation to generation.*

It was Saturday's class, the last of the week naturally, that I liked best. Everybody loved Saturday's class. It was jokey, it was approached lightly. It ended with a combination called "the door step," with each of us crossing the room, jumping, turning, recrossing and exiting by a *jeté* out of the door, which was opened by the teacher as we approached. From there you went home. We kids loved that.

Friday's class was impossible, Tuesday's difficult, the others okay. In those days, the Bournonville style, the great Danish contribution to ballet and the pride and at times in its history the sole reason for being of the Royal Danish Ballet, didn't interest me at all, never touched me, and I was never as good a Bournonville dancer as the others in my class. At least, that is what I was told. However, their definition of a Bournonville dancer didn't quite match my own, and to this day still doesn't. Perhaps the problem was that the teacher never engaged my imagination or made me see the artistic possibilities. Or perhaps he himself danced Bournonville in a rigid, limited manner.

I don't feel that Bournonville's ballets or his style should be treated as museum artifacts, to be danced exactly the way some teachers think they

---

*"Bournonville is not different because of any kind of old-fashioned or 'stylish' look, but because his steps are choreographed in a different way. He knew what was necessary to build the technique and physique, so he choreographed long enchaînements with musical phrasing which allowed the steps to be more interesting. He never composed a variation in class or on stage where the dancer would merely walk or run from one corner to another (in order to prepare the next phrase). He made the dancer dance at all times, even with the back to the audience." Kirsten Ralov, *The Bournonville School* (New York: Marcel Dekker, Inc., 1979), p. ix.

were originally performed. We are different dancers today from the dancers these works were made on, with differently proportioned bodies, differently developed, and with different physical abilities, and with different artistic goals. These old ballets should be danced with the present in mind — we should be reinvigorating them (yet without changing their basic form) creating them anew, not reconstructing them as if they were architectural plans. Are Shakespeare's plays acted as they were in Shakespeare's day (and who is the authority who can tell us how they were done?), with an imitation of the way the language was spoken, with the acting manners of that day? Of course not. In our own day we have seen that George Balanchine's ballets are danced differently from the way they were initially performed (and Mr. Balanchine was the first to make sure the works were altered over the years to keep them alive). The original impulse of old works will emerge if they are taken out of a frame and allowed to breathe in the air of the present.

The Bournonville technique, as many have pointed out, bears resemblance to Balanchine technique in its demands for intricate footwork, jumps, exposed open dancing, great technical finesse. It was years later, when I had settled in the United States, that I reinvestigated this style, taking Bournonville classes again and finding the material fascinating.

The Danes have a conflicted relation to this Bournonville heritage, for the fear is that it can stifle present creativity, that it can make the company seem a museum of nineteenth-century style and repertory. In an effort to invigorate the company's technical command, to make it equal to that of other major companies, Harald Lander just before his resignation as ballet master in 1951 brought Vera Volkova to Denmark to teach Russian technique and to overhaul the school's curriculum. A student of Agrippina Vaganova, the famous Russian teacher and theorist who had trained, among others, Galina Ulanova, she had been teaching and coaching in London, where her most famous pupil was Margot Fonteyn, and her Russian style was tempered somewhat by the English manner, making it somewhat restricted and less flamboyant. Stanley Williams was greatly influenced by her, and it was only later, when I had been away from her classes for some time, that I realized how much an effect she had had on me, both directly and through Stanley.

What Stanley was teaching was not the traditional, inherited style, but a way of dancing classical ballet that took account of the present, that was modern in feeling. It was a living method that held the possibility of exploration and of extension and variation of the classical technique.

What appealed to me about Stanley was his attitude: one of honesty, directness, and lack of fuss. Here was no grand manner, no parading — everything was clear, visible, unforced. There was no pretense, no fooling around, no unnecessary politeness. I always felt that Stanley just did what he wanted to do. He never tried to do more, and he never tried to fool me or tried to pretend that he had something great to offer. He just laid it on the line, as if he were saying, "This is what I've got; do you want it or not?" He also thought of dance as a profession, as a serious occupation, as something important and respectable.

There were teachers who came to class with hangovers, even drunk (alcoholism is an acute problem in Denmark and the company then was no exception — the Carlsberg brewery's second largest customer, after B&W Shipbuilders, was the Royal Theatre), and careless and sniggering about what they were doing. They made it all too clear that we students weren't especially interesting. And there among all these was a teacher who told us that there was point and reason to what we were trying to master.

Despite my inattention in most of my classes, my progress was rapid, and with that progress came competitiveness. By the time I was sixteen, the holdouts gave up and they grudgingly admitted I was talented, exceptionally talented, but that to fulfill my potential I was going to have to get to work.

While I was refusing to subject myself to real discipline and concentration, I knew I could maintain a certain level, and that level, though hardly the best I was capable of, was better than anyone else's. Basically, I was unfocused. With certain exceptions, dancers with talent are tempted to coast on their ability and not press their talent — they face the danger of becoming lazy and they have to fight that. It seems to go with the talent, this hazard, and often they need extra inducement to urge themselves ahead.

I remember the other talented boy in the class, a boy who had to work his butt off to do what came to me with ease. What he didn't have was the flair, but in many technical ways he was superior to me. He could work easily to both left and right, whereas I had to concentrate, especially to the left. I always stayed just at his level, perhaps a bit ahead, sometimes just behind, but he was the measure of what was acceptable, and that is all I bothered to maintain.

What now stands out as representative of my Danish training, and what I believe distinguishes it from all other disciplines, is a try for perfection in all aspects. It is an effort to make dance a continuous flow of smooth excellence. At the conclusion of class we would have a combination of steps that were to be mastered not as separate components but as a series, as an entity, no part more important than another, and mastery of one aspect was meaningless if the others were not executed equally well.

For instance, here is a combination that had turns in the air, *pirouettes*, beats, pulling in: six *entrechat-six*, open to *tendu* second, *grand pirouette à la seconde*, then pull in to *pirouette* in high *passé*, close fifth, then *double tour en l'air* to the knee.

It had to be done with constant specificity, perfectly executed: the pull in perfect, in the *six*'s good elevation, landing in a perfect fifth from the *six*'s, no hopping into *pirouette*, a high *passé*. And what made it all so interesting and challenging was that this must be right on the music (two eights).

There was only one way, the right way, and this was very Danish, this striving for constant excellence, with concentration all the way through. In Russia, the emphasis might have been on the highest jump, and just getting in as many turns as you can, and the highest double turns in the air, landing on the knee at the end, the most extreme effect. But here all was equal and no step sacrificed or merely indicated for the sake of another.

If any part was slightly imperfect, then all the rest was disregarded and you'd try and try again by yourself until it was perfectly done. And this, of course, was only one combination of the many we were given.

During my teens, the three most important male dancers in Denmark were Henning Kronstam, Erik Bruhn, and Flemming Flindt. Though a first-rate dancer, Kronstam was thought to be the one with the smallest talent among these three, but his great gift was that he seemed the most sensitive, the most poetic in performance, what John Gielgud is considered as an actor. He was the dream prince, the romantic hero: Albrecht, James, Romeo. The audience loved Kronstam, and everyone loved him too for being the one who stayed in Denmark, who stuck it out.

Erik Bruhn was the first male dancer to have international success after the war, and we'd wait for his periodic returns. Erik was the technical whiz, and he strove for perfection. Whenever he returned home, he'd have absorbed some touches from where he had danced. And when Nureyev defected, Bruhn attempted to alter his own style radically to include some of Nureyev's fierce manner and feats.

Flemming Flindt, too, took off for the world outside. Of the three, he was the most flamboyant, as if it was the immediate response of the audience that appealed to him. The big hand, the trick. And he'd return from appearances outside Denmark even more extravagant than before he left, bringing the folks back home a bit of Paris. To us kids in school it seemed that these guys came home when they needed money or had some extra time on their hands.

These three were such different dancers that they demonstrated the vast range of approaches to dancing. Of the three different approaches, the one that appealed to me was Erik's, and I thought he was the best. Flemming was his challenger, and he was named first runner-up among us students. I remember his Albrecht in one *Giselle* that was astonishing. My friends said this beat Erik Bruhn and I said no way, no way; maybe it was exciting, but it wasn't pure. And they looked annoyed. There you go, they said, with your purity. Purity isn't everything.

Henning was third, probably because we saw him every day. When those two other biggies would disappear, Henning would still be there.

Vera Volkova had put her stamp on all of them and had really extended their talent. Flemming was a student of Stanley's as was the next major male dancer to appear after these three, Niels Kehlet.

Kehlet was as different from each of them as they were from each other. Because he was small he was like a male soubrette, with an enormous light jump but with no emphasis on precision. In that way he was like Flemming. Kehlet tried for an international career and guested everywhere, but he never followed up. Even in his greatness, he was insecure, not certain himself that he would fulfill his promise. Often I think that it was just the luck of circumstances, such as timing and geography, that prevented him from becoming the sensation that Baryshnikov became several years later.

That world that lay beyond our borders. It was really Erik who gave us a sense of its large possibilities for a dancer, for he was our first dancer who achieved a huge international reputation, who would appear with companies in New York and London and Paris and Monte Carlo. He came back to us with the aura of that experience, with an authority that carried to his stage presence and stage command. Erik could capture an audience's attention by doing nothing; his very entrance would cause an audience to tighten their attention and their expectations. In my first years as a dancer, critics noted that I seemed to be imitating Erik Bruhn in my dancing, and indeed I was.

By the time of my graduation I was named one of the two most promising boys in my class. The graduation examination was held in the big main studio. Behind a long green table sat all the school faculty plus the theater administration and staff: every teacher, the doctor, the masseur, the director, the coaches, the conductor. Each of them had a ruled rating sheet with spaces for entering grades for musicality, physicality, intelligence, ability, proportion, pure talent.

Behind this row of judges, in the little remaining space and in the doorway, squeezed dancers, critics from abroad, dignitaries, some fans, dedicated hangers-on, but there was no audience per se, and no relatives of the students.

We did a long class, with extended center work, and at the conclusion of that I and another boy did solos, which were cheered by the impromptu group. It was almost embarrassingly obvious how successful this class prepared by Stanley Williams was.

But the success was less apparent to the rest of the staff, who were convinced we were all too un-Bournonville, and that Stanley was responsible. Stanley, who had been so proud of what we had accomplished, who was convinced that he had never had such a fine group, and then to be told this! To be told that his triumphant students were damaging the great Bournonville tradition, and that he was the instigator of this destruction!

I believe this response to his teaching was the crucial factor in his decision to leave Denmark and to accept George Balanchine's offer to teach in New York at the School of American Ballet, the official school of the New York City Ballet.

After graduation, I became an apprentice in the Royal Ballet, dancing in the corps, but I had no doubt I would become a full member of the company.

I thought I was a good partner and a strong one until a performance of Bournonville's *Far from Denmark*. In the corps, I had to lift the girl in the air and hold her there through the applause. Of the twenty boys, I was the one to lower the girl first. She looked at me in tight fury and said, "You need push-ups." After the performance I cried my way home, and the next day not only began push-ups, but bought a chest expander.

Two weeks before my official debut with the company in 1964, I made an unofficial debut in a work called *Garden Party* that Frank Schaufuss had made for two couples to excerpts from Glazunov's *Raymonda* music. Erik Bruhn had one of the two male leads, and when the other boy became ill five days before the first performance, I took over his part. That was not a particularly comfortable appearance, for I sensed Erik's apprehension at this young dancer, this kid was so big, dancing next to him as if they were equals.

My official debut, in a Hans Brenaa ballet called *Moods,* came when I was eighteen, and it began another education. I was entering the company as a full member in a solo role, though I would have to continue to appear in the corps. I've never been a good corps dancer: I keep bumping into the other boys, forgetting what comes next, totally out of sync. Surrounded by many I simply lose my concentration, wondering if I'm doing the step precisely the way the dancer next to me is doing it. I think a lot of it has to do with my size, my need to make my own space when I dance. I didn't like the feeling of being confined to two or three square feet. Being a corps member was the bane of my existence.

By then, I was living with Lise La Cour, a young dancer in the company. I had fallen in love with her when I was sixteen, but at that time she had been involved with someone else. I remained faithful, and a year later when she was free of that relationship I moved with speed. My mother had always treated me as an adult and since I had been self-supporting by virtue of the salary I received as a company apprentice she could raise no strong objection when I told her I was moving out to live with Lise. I was a very serious young husband with maybe not such an odd ambition for one so young — I wanted to be a father. One year after our marriage my son was born, a Prince Charming with tiny feet. The night of his birth I was dancing in Birgit Cullberg's ballet *Moon Reindeer*, and I named our son after the ballet's hero, Nilas. My son's fate was decided even then, maybe even before his birth. He *was* a dancer.

We were a very young family, too young it turned out, and our immaturity caused problems that ultimately became unresolvable.

In those first years with the company the roles given me were mostly from the modern repertory, and I danced in works by John Cranko, Kenneth MacMillan, and Frederick Ashton, and there were also ballets in the repertory by George Balanchine — I have especially happy memories of *Bourrée Fantasque*.

Moods, with Lise La Cour (© Rigmor Mydtskov)

Bagage, with Johnny Eliasen, Arne Beck, P.M., and Ib Andersen (© Rigmor Mydtskov)

Young Man Must Marry, (above) with Mette Hønnigen
(© Rigmor Mydtskov)

Le Loup, with Vivi Flindt (© Rigmor Mydtskov)

A Folk Tale, with Sorella Englund (© Rigmor Mydtskov)

The Three Musketeers, with, left to right: Jørn Madsen, P.M., Henning Kronstam, Flemming Ryberg (© Rigmor Mydtskov)

Apollo, with Anna Laerkesen (© Rigmor Mydtskov)

Apollo, with Inge Olafsen, Anna Laerkesen, Eva Kloborg (© Rigmor Mydtskov)

Apollo, with Ulla Skow and Marianne Walter (© Rigmor Mydtskov)

I began to have some celebrity because visiting choreographers, foreign critics, and company directors were noting my performances. Invitations for guest appearances began to arrive, and I had to pass these requests to the company director. Cranko invited me to join the Stuttgart company, Roland Petit wanted me to come to Paris, and there was an offer from the London Festival Ballet. The National Ballet of Canada asked me to guest. But the Royal Danish Ballet was not being particularly generous in giving me permission. Possibly, each invitation irritated them further.

In 1965, the company toured the United States, and though I was dancing in the corps, I also did the Greek dance in Vincenzo Galeotti's *Whims of Cupid*, the oldest performed ballet in any repertory. It was on that tour that I first danced on the stage of the New York State Theater, the home of the New York City Ballet.

At the end of that tour, Flemming Flindt was made ballet master of the company, succeeding Niels Bjørn Larsen. Flemming kept up the tradition of refusing any of the requests for me to guest outside the company. But he gave me roles in his new ballets, such as *The Three Musketeers*, *The Miraculous Mandarin*, *Gala Variations*, and *Le Jeune Homme à Marier*, a ballet with a libretto by Eugene Ionesco. Because roles in the established repertory were handed out on the basis of seniority, my classical repertory was limited — the *pas de deux* in Lichine's *Graduation Ball*, and the first and second movements of Balanchine's *Symphony in C*. For me there was no immediate chance of dancing *Giselle*, *La Sylphide*, *Swan Lake*, or *Sleeping Beauty*. And the chance at that repertory was another lure for me to guest elsewhere.

In 1967, I was promoted to principal dancer, the youngest dancer to be named a principal in the history of the company except for Erik Bruhn. I felt the honor, but there was something more I wanted.

That spring of 1967, I was assigned Balanchine's *Apollo*, and Henning Kronstam coached me in the role. The reviews said I was fair; I was suited to the part but would have to grow into it. The consensus: a promising first performance.

Balanchine had set this ballet first for the Royal Danish Ballet in 1930, two years after its premiere in Paris by Diaghilev's Ballets Russes, and my uncle had been the first Danish Apollo. At that time Balanchine had spent only six months with the company staging works from the Ballets Russes repertory, including his own, *Barabau*, and setting too his own version of Richard Strauss's ballet score, *The Legend of Joseph*.

Apollo had dropped out of the repertory but had returned in the fifties, when a number of Balanchine works were staged for the company. *Night Shadow* (now called *La Sonnambula*) and *Symphony in C* were especially successful. I believe that Balanchine had coached Kronstam in *Apollo* in the late fifties.

The summer following my debut in *Apollo*, Stanley Williams, who was by then teaching at the School of American Ballet, returned to Copenhagen to guest teach for the summer. My wanting to dance outside the company had focused on wanting to dance in America, and I hoped Stanley would be able to guide me on how to achieve that.

I asked to join him for supper at his hotel one Saturday night in the middle of the summer, and fired off question after question about what my chances were. His association was with the New York City Ballet, and he could only guess at what Ballet Theatre might do. If it came to Ballet Theatre Erik Bruhn might have something to suggest, so our conversation concentrated on George Balanchine and how best to bring me to his attention.

"If you come," he said, "I don't think you'll be taken as a principal, and frankly there is the chance that he won't even want you as a soloist. You might have to start in the corps. Balanchine makes up his own mind about ranking, and he'd only make that decision after he saw you."

"That doesn't bother me. For me, this is a matter of survival — I'll be destroyed if I have to stay here forever."

At that moment the waiter came to our table and told us there was a call from Vera Volkova for me. She had been searching for me for hours and had finally tracked me down. A small group from the New York City

Ballet was scheduled to open the day after next, on Monday, at the Edinburgh Festival. Jacques d'Amboise, who was to perform Apollo, had been injured, and the ballet would have to be dropped if they couldn't find another Apollo. Balanchine had asked John Taras, one of the company's ballet masters, to comb Europe for a replacement. The need was desperate, not only because of the opening but because it would be difficult to replace the work, given the small number of dancers who had come to Edinburgh.

A clear choice was Henning Kronstam, but he was unable to leave the country, and the other "European" Apollos were simply unavailable on such short notice. Vera Volkova named me as the savior when Taras turned to her with the problem. She had told Taras that my debut hadn't gone badly at all, and in fact had met with some success. On the chance, Taras had flown to Copenhagen to audition me. Would I come to the theater right now?

That was impossible, I told her. It was too late in the evening. This was no time for an audition. I was a principal dancer, remember; surely, if the Royal Danish Ballet had named me a principal I was a bit beyond "auditioning." Further discussion would have to wait for the morning.

All right, then it would be the morning, the first thing in the morning.

When I told Stanley, he was staggered by the coincidence. The chance had come to show Balanchine what kind of dancer I was, and we'd know soon enough if to his mind I was principal, soloist, corps, or not worth bothering about.

That next morning, Taras, Volkova and I met at the theater, and then Taras cabled Balanchine that rescue was on the way. We'd fly to Edinburgh immediately. I made one request: that Stanley must accompany me.

When we arrived in Edinburgh late that same afternoon, we were met by photographers and reporters. This was clearly a major event, and it was dawning on me that more was at stake than a chance audition for a restless Dane.

All the London critics had flown up, and there were headlines in the London papers that a young Dane was saving the New York City Ballet's

Overleaf: Apollo (© Martha Swope)

Apollo, with Suzanne Farrell (left: © Martha Swope; right: © Carolyn George)

Apollo, with Suzanne Farrell (© Martha Swope)

Apollo, (top) with Heather Watts; (bottom) with Karin von Aroldingen, Kyra Nichols, Heather Watts (© Martha Swope; overleaf: ©Steven Caras)

opening. All this news was being wired to Copenhagen; at home, I became an instant celebrity.

When Stanley and I went out for a stroll, I saw him smile at a thin, sharp-eyed, distinguished man who was walking with a light-brown-haired young woman. Stanley introduced me to George Balanchine and Suzanne Farrell, and Balanchine turned to Suzanne and said: "This is your Apollo."

She tilted her head, and gave me a slow once-over. We waited for her decision.

"Well, at least he's tall."

That night we met again in the theater where we were to perform, and Mr. Balanchine watched me without offering any changes for my solos, and making slight adjustments only in the *pas de deux*. The next morning I rehearsed with the rest of the cast, and everything seemed to go all right.

The company struck me as an odd one — I had known nothing like them, and I wondered at the style of American dancers. I'd never seen so many rules of correct ballet form broken. There was no emphasis on placement or correctness, and *all* the dancers neglected or didn't bother with precision. The emphasis was on energy and on movement itself, on timing and quickness. This was a completely different world, and just *how* different it took me a while to comprehend. These dancers showed a kind of seriousness and dedication that I guessed came from being members of an American ballet company. But the opening was a big success, and my effort was judged heroic. Proud that I hadn't let anyone down and had at the least allowed the opening to take place without the cancellation of an essential work, I arrived the next day for another rehearsal.

"Before we begin," Mr. Balanchine said, "you know, you do it all wrong." And then he tore apart my performance. Not much of what I had done had been right. Except maybe to show up. But he was very pleasant about it, and he showed me what he wanted by demonstrating, and he partnered Suzanne himself to illustrate how the *pas de deux* should go. In fact, he was wonderfully encouraging. At the beginning he asked me who had taught me the role, but then dismissed the question, for it was more important to start to revise the way I was dancing it.

By Wednesday's performance, he had made me reconceive the role, and he had reworked the way I danced it. Now I was dancing *his* version.

To summarize, he told me I was dancing *Apollo* too classically, and I was not giving it the suggestions of character and imagery that he had built in. Each step and phrase demanded a positive, clear accent and a strong attack. The whole role should be danced crisply and with firm definition, no slurring of any movement. My feet should move with the kind of force needed to punt a football or to sidekick it down a field. My legs were to be bent sometimes — they shouldn't be classically beautiful, but should be shaped to a charged effect. They could be thought of as powerfully made, abstract shapes. Don't always turn out, turn in.

Throughout the ballet, Apollo is exploring, testing possibilities. There are stabs and mistakes and awkwardnesses, but the movement is to be urgent, not tentative. I had been trying to make everything beautiful and grand, and he demanded shapes that looked grotesque but were packed with energy. He would show me what he wanted, and the best way for me to understand was to watch him.

At the end of the week, I still felt that this New York City Ballet world had nothing to do with the other ballet world, the world of *Giselle*s and of "big productions." And I still didn't know if Mr. Balanchine wanted me.

What I think now is that he recognized a very suitable partner for Suzanne. He liked the way we looked together. For my part, I was immediately interested, not so much in what he showed me, but I was interested in him, not the difference in the way of performing the steps, but the way he approached it all, the way he did it. I fell in love with this man.

He was so wonderfully natural. His approach, his attitude to his craft. This was an enormously great man. One eye on him and I knew what dancing was all about. He radiated knowledge and authority. He was never condescending, and he never pretended to know more than he did, yet, maybe there wasn't much he didn't know. These were the same qualities that had attracted me to Stanley Williams.

It was his clarity and directness about what he wanted — this concrete, sensible attitude went beyond what he did. This was a man who was sure and firm, but not driven or crazed or so wholly absorbed by dancing that he risked losing proportion.

What I did was listen, and I allowed myself to be instructed. I was passive through this experience.

On the plane back to Copenhagen I asked Stanley what I was supposed to do next. If Mr. Balanchine liked me, he said, he'd be in touch. At some appropriate moment he would ask Mr. Balanchine what he thought of me, but it would be wrong to become too insistent and too pressuring. That might have the wrong effect. Mr. Balanchine liked to make up his own mind. It would be best to remain calm and patient.

What Stanley could assure me of was that Mr. Balanchine had been impressed. "You see," he had told Stanley, "I changed everything for him, and he remembered everything."

So, I was returning to Denmark a celebrity, with a check and the assurance I had a memory.

Back in Copenhagen, I felt my world looked lifeless. In some way, my brief experience with Balanchine had left me baffled, but more importantly I was attracted to the new world of ballet that I had found. Patience was rewarded: two months later a telegram came. George Balanchine invited me to guest during the company's run of *Nutcracker* performances in December. Again, there was the trial of getting permission, but a request from Balanchine is not turned down lightly. Reason prevailed and permission was given.

I arrived two days before my debut with the NYCB, and as the Sugar Plum Fairy's cavalier, partnering Suzanne Farrell, I appeared once again on the stage of the New York State Theater. The critics were welcoming, and at the end of two weeks George Balanchine asked me to stay for another two weeks, to learn *Diamonds,* the concluding ballet of a tripartite evening called *Jewels,* and a ballet made especially for Suzanne.

My first reaction was that I had to return home to my family. It seemed to me I had been away a long time already, and I wasn't sure how far I could try the patience of the Danish Ballet. Luckily, Stanley was there to remind me this was the opportunity I had been begging for not so many months before. It would be foolish to refuse Mr. Balanchine now. But at the end of those second two weeks, I did go back to Copenhagen. Two months went by. The NYCB was beginning its spring season when the telegram came, this time inviting me to do *Apollo* in New York. The argument over the leave of absence was starting again, and my resolve to settle this question once and forever began to grow.

That spring I danced *Apollo* and *Diamonds* in New York, and partnered Suzanne in Balanchine's setting of Brahms's *Liebeslieder Walzer.* Jacques d'Amboise had a string of injuries that kept him out — and kept me in. I was learning ballets overnight and performing them the next day.

What I was slow to learn were American manners. When I'm uncomfortable I tend to appear overly formal and pointedly proper. This behavior seemed to me to display good manners and reserve. However, others thought me conceited, cold, unfriendly, and pompous (when they were being generous). Through Stanley I made one firm friend almost immediately, Robert Weiss, a young dancer with the company.

My performances went well, and Mr. Balanchine finally made me the offer I dreamed of, the offer that was unimaginable before Vera Volkova's call the previous summer. He wanted me to know that whenever I was free I could join the company, but he didn't want it to appear that he had stolen me from the Royal Danish Ballet. I couldn't deny that the Danes still wanted me, and I hesitated to make a complete break. For the next year and a half I was a jet commuter, spending more time in the air than rehearsing some of the ballets I danced. My schedule was a complicated one, what with meeting my commitments to the Danish Ballet and being an ever-present guest with NYCB.

There was another solution to this between-two-worlds dilemma, one that had been granted other Danish dancers. I applied to Flemming Flindt for a two-year leave of absence, or an indefinite leave. (Flemming had received this grant himself in previous years.) Such grants were at an end, he responded. Letting dancers drift away after the company had paid for their years of training and schooling depleted the whole organization. What was the point of the system except to maintain the company? As it was I was straining the company's resources by not being there when I was needed. Eventually I was given an ultimatum: either I stop this constant guesting in New York and settle down, or get out of the company for good. I was reminded that I'd lose my pension if I made the break now. (Erik Bruhn cautioned me about losing the future security of the pension that came with being a member of the Danish Ballet, and I knew he was talking feelingly on that, for he had given up the right to that benefit. He had been a member of the NYCB for two years, but he never felt comfortable there, and had returned to a more secure place with American Ballet Theatre.)

Long ago I had made my decision and now it was a question of acting on it. I gave my resignation, and in mid-1970 I told Mr. Balanchine I was free to join his company as a permanent member.

There was nothing easy in any of this but I was moving with the force of an urgent necessity. I was leaving my family and leaving the institution that had bred me. By now it was clear that my wife and I could not salvage our marriage, and I would be separated from my son for long stretches of time in any case (though we have spent summers together ever since). And for what? For the chance to dance somewhere else. It couldn't be reasoned out so easily and to think about what I was doing was to face the riskiness of it all. But with all that, I had never felt so relieved in my life. I felt free of some burden, and I had rid myself of it by making a strong, and perhaps blind, commitment. It was more than likely that I'd never dance in Denmark again, and I would be gone for I didn't know how long. But I would be living in that "movie" America I had felt for many, many years was my real home.

For the following two years, the Danish Ballet ignored my existence. The public did not feel that I had committed any act of betrayal, for they were used to complaining about the management of the company; and to some, it appeared that I had been driven out. At the end of that two-year period, there was a reconciliation, and Flemming invited me to guest with my former company, in Balanchine's *Apollo*. I was also offered my first *La Sylphide*, and appeared in Flemming's version of *Swan Lake*.

With my resignation from the Danish Ballet, all should have moved forward smoothly. After all, I had been bold and brave. But it wasn't so easy.

The spring gala in 1970 at the New York State Theater was the occasion for the premiere of a new ballet by Jerome Robbins, *Dances at a Gathering*. It marked Robbins's return to the company after a long absence, and a major return to ballet for him (though he had staged Stravinsky's *Les Noces* for Ballet Theatre a few years before). It was an important night in ballet history, upstaged slightly by Suzanne Farrell. A few days before, she and her husband, Paul Meija, had quit the company. The issues involved were complicated, and there are many versions of what happened, but that is someone else's story to tell. What this did though was to leave me without the dancer I was most at ease with (balletically), to leave me without a partner, and to leave me without a clear function and place in the company.

Symphony in C (© Martha Swope)

Diamonds, with Suzanne Farrell (opposite page and top left: © Paul Kolnik; top right: © Steven Caras; bottom: © Martha Swope)

Allegro Brillante, with Patricia McBride (© Martha Swope)

Allegro Brillante, with Suzanne Farrell (© Martha Swope)

Stars and Stripes, (left) with Merrill Ashley (© Martha Swope)

Don Quixote, with Karin von Aroldingen
(© Martha Swope)

Brahms-Schoenberg Quartet: Intermezzo, with Patricia
McBride (© Martha Swope)

Brahms-Schoenberg Quartet: Rondo alla Zingarese, with
Suzanne Farrell (© Martha Swope)

The Nutcracker, with Suzanne Farrell (© Martha Swope)

Swan Lake, with Suzanne Farrell (© Martha Swope)

CHAPTER TWO

Far from Denmark

*W*hen I first became a member of the New York City Ballet, Balanchine was not teaching the company class every day. When he resumed teaching daily he noticed that I was attending less and less.

My company participation extended only to the parts I had been assigned: most often *Diamonds, Apollo, Symphony in C, Nutcracker, Concerto Barocco, Liebeslieder Walzer*. I learned what I was told to learn but nothing more, and one of the reasons I absented myself from his classes was because I thought they were, to put it nicely, unconventional, and I was the most conventional dancer in the world.

I had never been asked to do only a ten-minute barre before and, as the first step in the center, a *double tour en l'air* to *grand plié*. I soon learned that the next day's class might consist of a twenty-five-minute barre with no *double tours* to *grande plié*, but half an hour of *pas de bourrée*'s, and at that point I thought *pas de bourrée* was just for girls.

The other reason I began avoiding his class was that he found me an easy target for ridicule. It was my neatness and try for cool perfection that seemed to irritate him, and when he imitated the way I looked dancing he made me look prissy and overrefined. He was devastating to me, and I felt humiliated in front of the whole company.

I couldn't keep exposing myself to this kind of embarrassment and hurt, so instead of this, the company class, given in the late morning, I took Stanley Williams's men's class at the School of American Ballet and I took another class outside of the company. Yet with all that, it didn't take me long to realize that Balanchine was no ordinary teacher, but a master constantly experimenting with his choreographic craft on *his* dancers — and how extraordinary his teaching points were!

The roles that I had been given I still performed, and what I wanted was a role created *on* me by Mr. Balanchine, but my first experience of Mr. Balanchine choreographing me was dismal. For the Fall 1970 season Mr. Balanchine decided to revive for the New York City Ballet a work he had first made in 1947 for Ballet Theatre, *Theme and Variations*, set to the last movement of Tchaikovsky's Suite No. 3, in G. Its first production was tailor-made for two great technicians, Alicia Alonso and Igor Youskevitch. For the new production, Balanchine made new choreography for the first three movements, and the fourth movement (the old ballet) featured the company's newest ballerina, Gelsey Kirkland.

Theme and Variations is a summation of classical ballet, one of Balanchine's statements on the classical idiom, and his extension of the classical vocabulary. In the new sections, the first three movements, he explored three other aspects of man's response to women. The first movement, "Elegy," opens with a barefoot boy, dressed in flowing blouse and pants, on one knee in a reverie. A phalanx of girls enters, in long chiffon dresses, barefoot too, hair loose, and the boy searches among them, is sought out by them, finds and loses the principal girl among them. This is a dance essay about mood, a dream, with implications of loss and regret, desire and guilt.

That boy was made first on me. Balanchine choreographed this movement in one day — actually, in two and a half hours. I was so busy kneeling and wandering and searching and running and being surrounded that I couldn't decide what I myself could add to the performance. There didn't seem to be any real dancing. This was the first time in my dance life that I was not being asked to do any steps, was asked to do a minimal amount of dancing, yet strive for a maximal effect. (Later, I learned that doing the minimal yet getting the maximal effect was practically Balanchine's motto.)

On the second day of rehearsal, Balanchine devoted himself to ridiculing my stiffness, formality, lack of expression, and general clumsiness. I was not merely terrible, I was inadequate and unusable. After that rehearsal, he asked me to his office.

There he said directly what he had been implying throughout the rehearsal: I couldn't do that section. I was simply no good at all in it. "You can't run." The section wasn't my style. I was out. What I could do — possibly — was the final section, "Theme." Now that was in the strictly classical style I knew something about. Standing in fifth position and all that.

I did not answer him back but I was furious and hurt. I simply couldn't manage to say anything, which was just as well since what I was thinking was best not said aloud.

A few days later, I was called to a rehearsal of "Theme" with Patricia McBride. Afterwards, Balanchine confronted me again, this time more casually, and asked me to talk with him in the hallway.

"Well, you know, dear, this isn't quite right yet."

"But this is exactly what you told me I could do!"

"Someday you'll be able to do this, but now you just can't do it. You don't do it the way it should be done. You have to practice, practice. You know I made this for Igor Youskevitch, and he could do all these things, *double tours*, *double pirouette*. Keep practicing, and one day . . ."

This clearly sounded as if he wanted to have me out of the way. He couldn't use me, though maybe there was some need in the company for a partner of my height and competence. I filled a tiny gap, but that was all, since obviously there wasn't anything in my dancing that interested him at all. The experience was a nasty one.

My patience and tolerance (at that age — I was about twenty-three — I had not much of either) were running out, for this view of my talents was too destructive to live with much longer. At a meeting I requested with the company director, Lincoln Kirstein, I told him that as far as I could see there was nothing in that "Elegy" section I couldn't do — there wasn't much to do in it anyway — and I could run around the stage as well as anyone in the company. What was wrong was that Mr. B. had no patience, and I was wrongly perceived and unappreciated. Lincoln was sympathetic and promised that soon I would be featured in a new production.

That turned out to be a rescension of Fokine's *Les Sylphides*, presented under its original title, *Chopiniana*. It was Balanchine's intention to rid the Fokine ballet of its atmosphere, so that its choreographic originality and first revolutionary impulse could be appreciated. Gone were the girls' long skirts and boy's artist's blouse, and the country cemetery backdrop. It was performed in practice clothes against a bare cyclorama. The boy's variation is not difficult in the conventional sense (no big tricks), and in fact the entire ballet, by paring down the dance to its expressive and nontechnical essence, is an essay in choreographic delicacy. This casting hardly healed my bruised ego. Dance critics were for the most part horrified at Balanchine's tamperings. To them the "cleaning up" had done away with the original ballet, and the case he seemed to be making was that Fokine's work was a prelude to his own. Anyway, whatever this *Chopiniana* did for Fokine or Balanchine, it certainly didn't do much for me.

My disorientation was no secret, and if anyone doubted it, all he'd have to do was overhear my conversations with my few friends whom I never stopped haranguing with complaints. Eventually, and with my concurrence, the news traveled to the administration of Ballet Theatre, and secret negotiations were begun on the recommendation of my close friend Christopher Allen. Erik Bruhn thought the change was what I needed. His own experience with NYCB had not been a happy one. It seems ironic now when the company's male roster is full of Danes, but in those days it appeared that the atmosphere of NYCB was not a healthy one for Danes.

Among the things I wanted to be certain of was that I could go on dancing *Apollo*, and ABT seemingly had the rights to perform it by virtue of an old contract, though their revival wouldn't be sanctioned by Balanchine, and they suggested that I stage the third act of Bournonville's *Napoli*.

Since I knew I was flirting with a decision stemming from frustration and anger and disappointment, I had to demand extravagant terms to justify it, to make the move seem reasonable. All these demands were finally met, and the negotiated contract was to be signed over lunch at an expensive French restaurant with ABT's director, Lucia Chase. What was impelling me toward making this move — a move which would negate my original intention in coming to America — was not unbridled ambition, or the need for fame, or a chance for glamour. It was revenge for my feelings of being condescended to, of being unappreciated and unloved, and for what I perceived as the lack of any faith in my capacity to learn and change.

I knew that once I left the New York City Ballet, I'd never be able to return. Now, at the last moment, with the contract before me and every expectation that I would sign, I had to face the truth that my reasons weren't good enough. Almost too late, I recognized that to leave for Ballet Theatre would be an admission of defeat.

I didn't sign the paper in front of me, and quite properly Lucia Chase got up and walked out of the restaurant. Christopher Allen, who had acted as my agent, swore that our friendship was at an end and followed her out the door.

It would be nice if we could protect our friends from our confusions. None of the participants in this debacle, including Erik Bruhn, spoke to me for months. They felt I had been leading them on, but I had been serious through it all, and it was the very seriousness that kept me from the final commitment. I had been acting out an option, and only when the reality was there in front of me could I know that it wasn't the right one.

I couldn't risk the loss of working with Balanchine, and from this minidrama I discovered that my commitment was deep and irrevocable, and the task was to live with it, and to make it work.

Not immediately, but some time after this, I got up my courage and cornered Balanchine. My situation would have to be clarified.

My point was simple: I told him that I had come to the United States to dance, that before then I had no real appreciation of his achievements or his exalted place in ballet. I learned these quickly though, and my ambition now was to dance his ballets. It was all I wanted to do. And I would do anything to make this possible. I was not an unwilling student, and I worked hard. When I did dance, I received good reviews, but the "when" was the problem. There was no point in arguing whether he was avoiding me or not. What was to be aired was why.

He answered me, bluntly and directly. "You see, dear, you don't seem to be interested. I never see you anywhere, not in class, maybe in O'Neal's restaurant. When people show interest, I use them. If they don't, I leave them alone. And you don't show interest."

I was shocked. We had been getting the wrong messages, and the

misunderstandings had deepened each day. Such misreadings are not un-
common between directors and dancers. If that was what my behavior was
suggesting, then I had to change my behavior, which certainly didn't rep-
resent my true attitude. I had been digging my own grave. And did my
Danish sangfroid add to this impression of not caring? I'm accused all the
time of being cool, self-possessed, distant, whereas I know I'm full of energy
and passion. How does this come about, this disparity between how I'm
perceived and how I feel? Bored? I'm never bored. Impatient, yes. Angry,
yes. But bored?

I told him all this, and his answer was in that case I had to change my
attitude, and show him that I was willing to work hard, to concentrate and
to behave with maturity. It was now up to me to prove to him my
seriousness and determination. If I succeeded, he'd let me do anything I
wanted.

It was this conversation that was the turning point in my career with
the NYCB, and though the results took some time to manifest themselves,
the atmosphere altered immediately. No longer would Mr. Balanchine disdain
to say hello, but smiled and welcomed me, even from a distance, with me
smiling and bowing my way around. It felt as if we had become friends.

In June of 1972, the company put on its Stravinsky festival, Balanchine's
tribute to his most celebrated associate, and a tribute to the greatest
choreographer-composer partnership of this century. It was to be a week's
worth of ballets, many of them created for the occasion by Balanchine,
Jerome Robbins and John Taras. The highest anticipation was focused, of
course, on Balanchine's new ballets.

The opening-night program (June 18, 1972) included three new Balanchine works: Sara Leland and John Clifford danced to a rediscovered
short piano piece, and then there were two works that have proved to me
major additions to the company's standard repertory, *Symphony in Three
Movements* and *Violin Concerto*. In the latter, I was among the principals with
Karin von Aroldingen, Kay Mazzo, and Jean-Pierre Bonnefous.

It was during the making of *Violin Concerto* that Balanchine first worked with me closely, and I suppose his choreography is partly a statement of his concept of me as a dancer. It is also a role that stretched me as a dancer. I remember that in the rehearsals he was slightly testy, but despite this, every once in a while he was impressed with me. I knew that here was a great challenge, but I trusted myself to meet that challenge.

Violin Concerto was my chance to show that I could dance "Balanchine." I knew that I could, and now I would prove it to him. He would demonstrate a passage and I would dive into it with enthusiasm, not only mastering what he was teaching but working it through, extending its implications, playing with its accents. I'd go for it, salt-and-peppering the steps. This energy and intensity produced energy in him. Once he saw that he had captured my intensity and interest, that I was devoting my gifts to his work, he gave still more, and the experience gave me an incredible high because I felt he trusted me. And the more he trusted me the less specific he would be. He'd come to a rehearsal with the start of an idea — "Something like this, dear" — and sometimes he would say when I'd improvise around it, "That's exactly right, that's good," and sometimes he'd say, "Well, could be done that way too, but . . ." Then he'd get up from his chair and show me. He made me feel as if I were collaborating with him, and in fact he considers this whole process of making ballets a true collaboration between the creator and what the body of the dancer can do — the better the body, the better the collaboration.

The central section was made up of two consecutive *pas de deux*'s, and I think this pairing had never been done before. The first, for Karin von Aroldingen and Jean-Pierre Bonnefous, I think of as raw and energetic and sexual, and the other for Kay Mazzo and me was romantic. The final gesture in our *pas de deux* looks almost sentimental: I cover her eyes with one hand as she leans backwards against me and open the other arm out before us. Balanchine's directions to us were "Make it look like an elephant trunk, and then move out your hand as if you're asking for money."

Perhaps Balanchine was playing off Kay's dark delicacy and vulnerable appearance against my stolidity. He used us together also in another work for the festival that has entered the repertory, *Duo Concertant*. In both these, he made me move with small steps, the steps in contrast to my size, with a great deal of small-scale precision and sharpness. I had never been shown this way before.

Critics have said that my breakthrough as a dancer with a nameable character came with the Stravinsky festival. By then Balanchine had formed some idea of my dancing, of how to use me, and though it wasn't honed until he actually began choreographing on me, the idea was already there.

There was another element at work here. Choreographers do have stylistic concerns, are interested in working on specific problems at certain times. There is a choreographic coherency, a pattern that can be recognized over a period of time, and I was fitting into some current concern of Balanchine's. This may have had to do with scale and size, and contrasts and oppositions and even emotional reverberations. So, I became a vehicle for certain of his ideas at that time. In *Violin Concerto* and *Duo Concertant* Balanchine had explored aspects of my dancing that were a revelation to myself and maybe even to the audience. This is what the dancer most wants: to have a choreographer "create" him, to show him as the unique, special creature he is. Balanchine, of course, has done it for many, many dancers, and there are countless celebrated examples of his match of dancer and choreographic passage. Some that come quickly to mind are Helgi Tomasson's solo in *Le Baiser de la Fée*; Violette Verdy's solo in *Emeralds,* or Verdy in *La Source*; Merrill Ashley in *Ballo della Regina*. Great choreography, statements of a master, and also descriptions of dancers.

In choreographing for me, he guessed and gauged what I could contribute, and he extended the contribution when he saw what my participation and comprehension could be like. And he saw too, I think, my readiness to put my talent to serving his vision. There is an electric moment when the dancer and choreographer are in synchrony, when the idea is so clear, and the dancer catches the choreographer's intention so easily that they seem to be working together with total logic.

And the result of all this work was a happy surprise. During the actual

Violin Concerto, with Kay Mazzo (these pages and overleaf: © Martha Swope)

Violin Concerto, with Kay Mazzo (© Martha Swope)

Violin Concerto, with Lourdes Lopez (© Steven Caras)

making you go so quickly that you don't quite know what you have made until you are finished — really not until you're out of the studio and on the stage.

In *Duo Concertant*, there are actually four participants: the pianist and violinist as well as the two dancers. The dancing isn't continuous: sometimes the dancers stand by the piano, merely listening, then the dancers are urged to move, alone, and then together, the man inviting the girl's participation. Their space is limited by the simple fact that the piano and violinist share the stage. The dancing is intimate and small-scaled, beginning as a clear response and match to the music, and progressing to suggestions of some personal drama. The last section is celebrated for its opening stage picture. The stage is in blackness except for a small, empty pool of light. The girl enters her upstretched right hand into this light and then withdraws it. *Duo Concertant* is one of Balanchine's tenderest works and on its tiny scale it is a massive statement of the relation of music and dance. After the premiere, Balanchine embraced Kay and me and told us the ballet was ours.

Balanchine had brought me to discover how I could vary, extend and increase the range of the way I danced. And what he made me give up was any fear of looking inadequate or awkward. It was this very lack of fear, the willingness to try anything, that he seemed to like in me. What he was urging me to, what he was allowing me to discover, was my own way of moving. It was my true personal manner, a frame for further exploration (a way of existing on stage that was the sum of my physique, training, character, philosophy, temperament). I was becoming less rigid by becoming more particular, and he had pushed me to this. I had found a way of behaving more fully on stage. More of myself was implicated in the performance. I was altered as a dancer, for there was simply more of me, imaginatively.

I discovered how to make dancing be a creative act.

Having noted some roles that Balanchine made on certain dancers, I have to add the caution that when the role is danced by someone else, there are usually changes in the choreography. Balanchine is no fool: he knows that if he sticks to a one-and-only, first, original version, his ballet might grow tired-looking and stultifying. He knows the only way his ballets, even though they are acknowledged masterpieces, will survive is if dancers look good in them. And to make dancers look good, Balanchine will alter the choreography, if necessary. He'll adjust to bring out a dancer's special qualities, knowing full well that the total structure can withstand one dancer's exit and another's entrance if he makes slight adjustments. But you have to have a real ballet to sustain this, a ballet with a solid structure and a real idea. I believe he is absolutely right to be flexible about such changes: it gives his work organic life.

Also, as a ballet master, he is concerned with increasing his dancers' range, and so he will also cast "against type" — an *adagio* role, for instance, for a dancer with an *allegro* technique, or give to a young dancer a role that requires a sense of emotional maturity. Only by performing a role often will a dancer learn how to master it. Within a season, a ballet will be danced with different solos for different dancers, and there is no correct version (though critics might prefer one to another), just variations, so to speak, on variations.

The steps are not holy — it is the shape of the entire work, the artistic sense of the whole that matters. The ballet has its own integrity, and good dancers learn what aspects of the work they can vary and what they can't. Also, they have to work with their own capabilities: they are limited by them (certain steps might not be within their physical capacity or play to their strengths) and they can be extended by them (in fact, their strengths might enhance the part, bring to it an extra technical facility that might be inherent in the conception). Of course, dancers coach each other in roles, but dancers know (or should know) not to imitate another dancer's idiosyncrasies. They will have to find the role for themselves before mastering it.

When I was asked to do the danseur lead in Balanchine's *Divertimento No. 15* (to Mozart), I asked Erik Bruhn, who had been noted for this part

Coppélia (© Costas)

Coppélia (left: © Martha Swope; right: © Costas)

Tchaikovsky Suite No. 3, with Kyra Nichols (© Steven Caras)

Tchaikovsky Suite No. 3, with Merrill Ashley (© Steven Caras)

Who Cares?, (right) with Darci Kistler (left: © Martha Swope; right: © Steven Caras)

Duo Concertant, with Kay Mazzo (these pages and overleaf: © Martha Swope)

when he was with the NYCB, to coach me. He came to a rehearsal studio on a Monday, the day off, and in the midst of one of Erik's demonstrations, Balanchine walked in. We stopped, he noticed what we were about, he turned around and went out the door, and we continued.

Without anything being said, I was struck by the danger of being taught not the ballet but Erik's mannerisms, Erik's particular approach to the role. Either I found my own approach, or I was coached by the choreographer. Out of my embarrassment to be found being taught by a dancer no longer with the company, I studiously avoided using anything Erik had shown me, though I probably would have liked to.

The common idea is that Balanchine is a woman's choreographer, and "Ballet is woman" is the axiom associated, tiredly, with Balanchine. Yes, I think Balanchine does prefer to choreograph for women because he prefers to look at women, and because there is the added dimension of *pointe* work, but the roles I've danced have all had fascinating challenges, and I am proud of the wonderful parts he has made for me. Some great male roles include Oberon in his *Midsummer*, and another role made for Edward Villella, Harlequin in *Harlequinade*, *Prodigal Son*, Melancholic and Phlegmatic in *Four Temperaments*, and so on. Nonetheless, the list of female roles is longer (though the list would be equal in quality and importance).

Men have more fixed, and preconceived, notions of themselves than women do (or is this just a statement about male dancers?). Men are less vulnerable and less malleable than women. Balanchine feels this flexibility and possibility of women, their generous ability to give of themselves, and what he experiences from men is resistance, inflexibility.

When I was making my ballet *Sonate di Scarlatti*, which has equal male and female forces, I felt the joy of working with the girls, and I felt, too, the obstinacy and truculence of the boys. The contentiousness gives another energy that I relish and that I know full well from my own rebelliousness, but for getting from a dancer exactly what you want, the female dancer will catch the idea more quickly and be more patient. Perhaps this psychological difference comes from the way girls and boys perceive ballet; perhaps the boys feel they must resist the whole process. There is an unannounced reluctance before it all. Maybe. Being a male dancer, I am fairly expert with what a man can do in dance, and working with women in dance is novel and offers the greater area for creative exploration for me.

With the bromide of Balanchine and women, what is noted next is Balanchine's musicality. In truth, his musicality should only be discussed by another musician, and my opinion is nonexpert. But as a dancer I have seen that he knows innately when and when not to choreograph to the music, and to let the audience just listen to music without the added business of the dancers moving. Not all music is suitable for choreography: some music supports dance, some is too overpowering. Balanchine knows what to pick and what not to pick.

His way and approach to music, of fitting dance to a score, has changed over the years. The earliest Balanchine work still performed is *Apollo*, and he was twenty-five when he made it. The dance is all on what you hear. The work is choreographed to the melodic line, primarily. In this way, *Apollo* seems less like the sophistication Balanchine exercises in his later works — less complex in its relation to the music. It might be that his method is very different today: setting dance in counterpoint to the music, or leaving out material, or gliding over it. The main thing to remember is that the piece itself, his particular response to the piece, will dictate how the work will be made.

In working with Balanchine, you learn that he actually says very little by way of explanation, and allows the dancer to find his own way of dancing a role and his own relation to the character of the music. Again, the music will provide the key to a role, to the whole character of how you are to dance it. This is beyond the business of counting and hearing the music; it has to do with feeling the shape and size of the sound, of matching musical scale to dance scale. I come to think that good ballet is made up ninety percent music and ten percent dancing.

Other than the steps, nobody explained to me what I should be doing at any point, or who I was, or what I was supposed to do. And when there

Orpheus (© Steven Caras)

Orpheus, with Karin von Aroldingen (© Martha Swope)

Orpheus, with Adam Lüders (© Steven Caras)

Chaconne (© Steven Caras)

Coppélia (© Steven Caras)

Bournonville Divertissements (© Costas)

Bournonville Divertissements, with Merrill Ashley
(© Steven Caras)

Afternoon of a Faun (© Steven Caras)

Afternoon of a Faun (© Delia Peters [NYCB])

Robert Schumann's "Davidsbündlertänze," with Heather Watts (© Steven Caras)
Vienna Waltzes, with Kay Mazzo (© Martha Swope)

The Magic Flute, New York City Ballet production (© Steven Caras)

Chaconne, with Suzanne Farrell (© Costas)

was nothing to do, in a *pas de deux*, for instance, while the girl was dancing and I was standing cavalierly to one side, I'd make poses. In *Concerto Barocco*, in which the boy appears only in the middle, *adagio* section, I do some lifting and leading about but not much actual dancing. The more I listened to the music, the stronger my conviction grew that the less I did, the less mannered and pointed became my performance; the less insistent I became about my presence, and in fact the more invisible I felt myself, the clearer (oddly) the role became. I don't "exist" in *Barocco*, and in a way I hide behind the girl. To take it a step further (just one little step), one could consider that the girl conjures up this shadowy man just to lift her a few times. It is a mood of absence, and the music suggests this mood.

A dancer has to learn how to stand on stage, to do nothing, and yet hold the attention of some three thousand people. What you do is *feel*, and you stay almost nervously alert to what is happening around you. You don't act, you don't lose your concentration, you don't make yourself nonpresent. What you do is know where you are. Listen to the music, respond in your mind to where the other dancers are. Be aware of your body, of what it is doing (the picture of yourself that has been enforced by the mirror of the rehearsal room — it has fixed in your mind your control over what you look like, especially now when there is no mirror, when the audience is the mirror).

Agon, made in 1957, is the supreme example of George Balanchine's modern works, and in my early years with the company it was the work I most wanted to perform in. Of course he said no then, absolutely no. *Agon*, he explained, was a modern work, and it was still beyond me. My dancing was too severely classical for that work.

"But," I insisted, "I can do modern classically, neoclassical, right?"

When I was finally allowed to rehearse the *pas de deux*, he watched and was openly surprised.

"You know, I didn't know you could dance like this."

"I could always do this. You just didn't want to know."

"You didn't show me, dear," was what he offered as an explanation.

I think now that what made the difference is that I had learned the temperament of the music, though there was no difference in my ability "to do the steps."

Perhaps the furthest I have gone in asking to dance in a Balanchine ballet came during the preparations for the Ravel festival, in the spring of 1975. Balanchine had asked me (though this wasn't really a question) if I would be in his setting of *Schéhérazade*, and quickly I said yes, but when the rehearsal schedule was posted, the male dancer listed was Edward Villella. I knew this called for another of those hallway heart-to-hearts. I pounced at the first opportunity.

"It isn't as if I asked for *Schéhérazade*. You asked me, and now there is Villella's name on the schedule, so what happened to me?"

"Well, dear," he said, "I have to give all my dancers a chance, and Eddie is really senior to you, and you have another ballet."

"With all due respect, Mr. Balanchine, I'm here in this country and in this company because of you, and there are just so many new ballets by you. You shouldn't just drop me from one and give the role to someone else."

"What can I do? There is only one more piece that I am doing, *Tzigane*, a solo gypsy number for Suzanne Farrell, with some girls coming in at the end. That's all that's left, just little piece for her."

"Okay, that's fine. I'll be in that."

"Oh no, dear, you see, there's no man in this thing. Just a woman's solo really. The corps girls don't really do anything."

"I want to be in it if that's the only thing left. It's okay, I'll come in with the girls and sweep the floor in front of them, or behind them. I'll be scraping the back curtain. Don't worry, it will be good."

For a week, he barely acknowledged me, but I was listed for *Tzigane* rehearsals. It can only be ascribed to luck that *Tzigane* remained in the repertory while *Schéhérazade* didn't, though my contribution cannot be counted as one of the reasons. I just about make it on stage before the end, but I enjoy myself in that short time.

Agon, with Suzanne Farrell (above and overleaf: © Martha Swope; opposite page: ©Steven Caras)

Overleaf: Agon, with Suzanne Farrell (© Steven Caras)

Balanchine's strength comes from a mix of an ability to translate the images he sees into balletic form, and to work with dancers not by molding them to the idea but knowing how these particular dancers can embody these images from their own strengths and dance personalities. The genius enters in, perhaps, in that these images are so strikingly worth translating. But he is not an obsessed fanatic, and when choreographing he has a casual, easygoing approach, an undemanding attitude.

For his ballet to Robert Schumann's *Davidsbündlertänze*, he chose eight dancers, Suzanne Farrell, Heather Watts, Kay Mazzo, Karin von Aroldingen, Jacques d'Amboise, Adam Lüders, Ib Andersen, and me. We were selected because he knew exactly the kind of ballet he was making (you could call it because of its small cast a chamber ballet), and he knew he needed not steps but he needed dancers who would express best the feelings and thoughts, the images he was concerned with. All of us, *his dancers*, are personalities, and he knew beforehand what our effect would be. This ballet seems to involve images that are in soft focus, as if it were all blurred and the audience is meant to "sense through" the work. Nothing is absolutely clear, but suggested, nervously, with anxiety.

Most times Balanchine is a very spontaneous choreographer, though when inspiration doesn't come, and there might be an hour and a half remaining in a two-hour rehearsal period, he'll say, "Let's go to lunch."

Other times he'll walk in and say, "Let's start. Now you go there, and you go there." Fifteen minutes later he will have finished a whole section. Or he will come in and sit at the piano with our pianist, most often Gordon Boelzner, and discuss the score for a time, and then walk over to the dancers and talk with us about music generally, or this particular piece of music, what this ballet might be like, give us a biographical sketch of the composer, for twenty minutes. Then, for some twenty minutes more he'll work on steps that will take seconds in performance and conclude with "That's enough for today!"

With my settling into the company came an appreciation of Balanchine as a teacher, and it was in class we came to terms with each other. His methods are direct, and in his lack of shortcuts, his methods are very demanding. His class is not meant to *maintain* our condition, to keep us tooled up and in trim. His class is meant to *extend* our abilities as dancers, and to work on what the company needs might be — he might be concerned with some companywide slackening he has noticed in our performances in a specific technical area. Every other company has teachers who maintain the company, but not the NYCB. It is as if Mr. Balanchine expects his dancers to take care of themselves, to keep themselves in good condition by doing their own barre, or if need be by going to take an additional class somewhere else.

Dancers elsewhere are used to waking up each morning and going off to a teacher who gives a class that I would liken to a massage. Every dancer would like to have a gentle massage in the morning, but with Mr. Balanchine you have to arrive in his class prepared for everything to be asked of you. (A friend's ballet axiom is "Proper prior planning prevents poor performance.") For a Balanchine regimen you have to keep your body in a ready condition, and when you leave a class given by Mr. Balanchine or by Stanley Williams, you feel frustrated, not uplifted, because you have been asked to extend yourself beyond what you think your limits are. You haven't been made to feel wonderful and perfect. Most teachers tend to make you move slowly, without energy, slowly building you up, worrying over some minuscule perfection. You leave their classes *feeling* as if you've mastered the great secrets of the universe. There is a difference to be made between real teachers and people who give class. There are highly esteemed teachers who have never produced a dancer — they soothe and comfort, flatter their students, offering them a course in the philosophy of dance and personal coaching in technical matters that have nothing to do with getting on stage and showing dancing to the public. Real teachers are devoted selflessly to producing dancers, and do not press their ego on or make themselves out to be gods to their students. This is a devotion and self-abnegation beyond me.

After Balanchine's class you hurt and cramp, but then when you get on stage, you are prepared to dance — at least mentally, and later, physically.

The first two years in the company can be painfully trying for all new members, even if they are graduates of the school. You get tendinitis, your knees give way, the stress on turnout is almost brutal. And there is the possibility of serious injury for a dancer who does only Balanchine repertoire, because of its enormous demands. There have been casualties among the dancers, and those who have shied away perhaps too early, for I believe after the initial shock, the training proves its value.

Dancers and writers often talk of Balanchine's stress on speed, speed and clarity. But my sense of his true priority, of what he is working for, is different. The word I'd give it is *energy*. Energy can be fast or slow, but what Balanchine is demanding is that all parts of the dancing body be energized. There are no dead or resting limbs. Everything is active. Someone can be speedy and quick and still be dead. Speed in itself is not the point, though it is required. In *adagio*, Balanchine asks for an energy that is slow, slow but intense, and full. Whenever you move your arm or your legs, you are saying this is my arm, these are my legs, and I am putting them there.

The other thing I like in Balanchine's classes is his trust in himself. Teachers often think they have to give good combinations: "I have to come up with a good class so the students will feel comfortable and they'll say this is a good class." With Balanchine he'll come in to a class and do an abbreviated barre and then go to center. And there for one hour he will work on three steps, and these will be simple steps, but it is what he gets out of those steps that is important. Every once in a while, he brings to class some gimmick, and that's when he's working on a new ballet and is using the class as a testing ground. But when there is no choreographic project, his approach to the class and teaching is simple. He'll try a small jump and you'll do it twenty-five times over, and for ten minutes you'll do it very slowly, and then he will increase the speed. After twenty minutes of repeating this step, you'll find yourself exhausted, but you'll also have increased your mastery, and your body will have been schooled to do the step perfectly.

Sometimes he'll arrive twenty minutes late, and in the remaining forty minutes he'll pack in the whole class, with every step in the book. Or he'll come to class with a story that he has to share with us about dancers he's worked with, or what Diaghilev was really like, or a joke he has heard from his doorman, or his thoughts about politics. His stories all have morals, and one of his favorite lessons for us is that it is right and fitting that we as dancers give ourselves fully without holding back in class and in performance. Why are you saving yourself? he will ask. Stop preparing for the future. You might not have a future, you might be run over by a bus. So do it now, with everything you have. Give all of yourself now.

When he invited me to give company class, he warned me not to go to class with ten astonishing combinations just to show off my wonderful ideas and how creative I was. "You aren't there to give them a dance to do, to give them dancing lessons. You are there to make them feel the steps in their own bodies. The more they feel the correct way of doing each particular step, the closer they come to their own mastery and the more they will benefit."

It is that simple, and the simplicity and directness of this method is why I regard him as a terrific teacher. He presents no brilliant system, filled with tricks and notions and theories and refinements, but he has a trust in the power of the classical vocabulary.

Balanchine in class and in his ballets is asking for liveliness, the active presence of a dancer. He asks that you show your interest, your devotion, your joy in what you are doing. And he asks that you show that dance is your life, that your life, your act of living is dance.

CHAPTER THREE

Partners and Friends

hough the English I had learned in school gave me a base for what I needed to get around New York, the classical dance vocabulary, presumably international, that I had learned didn't really prepare me for the constructions, idioms, and local intonations of NYCB dancing. In fact there was little in my training, in what I saw in Denmark or on my travels, that prepared me for the kind of dancing that I found with the NYCB. It was a dance language I recognized but the accent was strange, and the values so different from the relatively rigid ones I had learned in Denmark.

It wasn't that I judged the dancing terrible or really made any judgments at all — the dancers I watched were so foreign to me that I couldn't understand what they were trying to do or why they were doing it. I wondered how I would ever mix in. I could never be an American dancer, and I supposed there were enough works in the NYCB repertory to carry the kind of dancer I was, but certainly I couldn't dance the way American male dancers were dancing. I was willing to learn anything, but I couldn't change my temperament and my physical shape and the way I thought about dancing.

One difference that immediately struck me was the way space was covered. I remember watching Jacques d'Amboise move across the stage with speed, but also with something else more amazing; he moved with a gradually expanding sense of scale, covering with ease in a few bounds the whole breadth of the stage — it appeared that he grew physically with each jump, and the dance image it created suggested the human form grown enormous, big enough to dominate the whole earth.

The dancer who confused me most, and whom I began watching with growing intensity over the years, was Edward Villella. NYCB was supposedly a company without stars, but Villella was a star and in a particularly American way. What I saw was rough-edged, overwhelming energy, full-out brio and excitement. None of his dancing was clean, in the old-fashioned sense that I had been bred in. He was a magnificent athlete, a fantastic animal, but with an American elegance and refinement. Here was someone with city street energy, who hadn't been brought up in the tradition-bound, sheltered, directed, somewhat protected environment that I had. One benefit it gave him was real freedom to define for himself how to use the academic dance vocabulary.

What I had been used to valuing was careful drawing and detailing dance, in the way I tried to make and shape my dancing. This included proper body alignment in all positions, keeping the correct shape while moving, soft landings. Villella's dancing was not hindered by these kinds of concerns, and it made no difference in the world, or rather, this couldn't be held against him, for I had never any doubt that he was a great dancer. What I had to learn was to stretch and redefine my conception of dancing.

So, he totally baffled and awed me, by defying all the rules of everything I had been taught was classical ballet. I was intrigued with this mystery, and his effect on the audience was proof positive of the enormous power of his dancing. Villella was undeniable. I saw him fly through the air, turn blindingly fast, increase and decrease speed with unbelievable facility. I saw an intensity and electricity that threw everything before it, and that made new rules for itself.

Balanchine has firm ideas about which roles suit big dancers and which small ones. Therefore, I've never had a real chance at many of the roles he made for Villella, in such works as *Harlequinade*, or *Rubies,* or Oberon in *Midsummer*, or *Tarantella*. During Baryshnikov's time with the company, Baryshnikov was given these roles that Balanchine sees for compact men who have the bodies of gymnasts. And I envy these roles, and I wouldn't mind very much even failing at them. What I'd like is the chance, for it isn't so much that I can or can't do them, it is that I'd like to see how they feel, and I'd like to be asked to meet the demands they make. The crossover roles have been *Apollo* (d'Amboise, Villella, Baryshnikov, and I have all danced that) and Baryshnikov and I have done *Orpheus*. In that I had the big-sized cast, Baryshnikov the physically slighter.

Villella and I have both done *La Source, Donizetti Variations*, and *Raymonda Variations*; in effect, I saw him do these ballets before I tried them, and they are works I still struggle and feel uneasy with. My performance of *Donizetti*

Variations came when no one else was available, and though I didn't know the role, Mr. Balanchine knew I was a fast learner and would be able to master enough of it so that my performance would be passable. I agreed to do it on one condition: that this not be my only performance of the role. "Certainly," he agreed, "it's just like Bournonville, you'll do it a lot." In forty-five minutes I learned the ballet, and left out only the male variation for lack of time for a thorough warm up. But for some years I was never asked to do the ballet again, and don't ask me why not (truthfully, I guess I actually know). *La Source* and *Raymonda* require pure classical dancing, and they are not constantly, or even frequently, in the repertory — they come and go, so just when I feel that I'm about to conquer their difficulties, they are left out of the repertory and I lose the momentum of the progress I'm making. Sometimes I feel defeated by these works. The biggest problem is stamina, for they are truly murderous if danced fully. By now, I've developed a mental block against them, and I give a passing grade to my performances of these works but wouldn't say that these were among the ballets I excel in. Perhaps, I've read the critics too often, or believed them too much.

I think this stamina, this ability to build to the breaking point (maybe beyond), to get stronger and bigger, is what Balanchine liked about Villella, for the works he made for him, especially the trifle *Tarantella* and the major *Rubies,* are equal killers.

Edward Villella is one of the two most American dancers I know — he could have been bred nowhere else, in no other country on this globe. The other is Suzanne Farrell, and the reason I was invited to join the NYCB was that I made a good partner for her.

Though Balanchine does not encourage steady partnerships, Suzanne and I have established a reputation as a duo. Our ease and comfort with each other was immediate. I'm tall and so is Suzanne, and we both dance with spacious, ample movement and gestures. We believe in the pressure of performance, that what happens, happens before an audience. Suzanne is a dancer who likes to take risks, to surprise the audience, to highlight the unexpected, and to dance with seemingly spontaneous reaction to the music. Indeed, she has her own versions of her roles, even multiple versions of the same role, and I won't find out which one she has in mind until we are on stage.

As a partner, I have to watch her with a different kind of concentration than I need for other dancers, for she is totally unpredictable and sometimes her performances veer toward the eccentric and fantastic.

She has been quoted as saying she likes to challenge me, and I do feel that challenge. That comes from technical strength which allows her to take risks and chances: altering to off-balance, making an extra turn, deepening the *penchée*, shifting an accent. To be able to do this, you have to be terribly secure, and very strong technically — or just plain talented — sure of the dynamics of a role, sure of what you can change without destroying the ballet or making a fool of yourself.

No dancer is perfect in all things, and Suzanne is a dancer whose methods and manner I had to learn. Where her strengths were and where she was less secure, where I could be of help and where I should get the hell out of the way. As soon as I've learned what she is going to do, I will know just when to aid her so that her performance will be seamless. I'm not there until she needs me, coming along at the last minute. In our first appearances I made mistakes, and I learned her skills slowly. What I had to learn was to anticipate her spontaneity, though this seems a paradox. She is a creative dancer, the most marked individualist in ballet.

When I first danced with the company, I had a crush on Suzanne. She was beautiful, sexy, fascinating, so self-contained as to seem unknowable. She was friendly, polite, but distant; not exactly withdrawn but you knew quickly she was someone who was solitary. She couldn't have cared less about me. I felt she was treating me like a puppy. She was the sophisticated lady and I the Danish provincial. She was Garboesque. Yet there wasn't anything unpleasant or chilling about this; she just didn't seem to be someone who needed friends to reassure her or to instruct her. What you sense after knowing her even a short time is her great integrity and dedication to dance. She makes the final decisions and she goes her own way, very sure of what she knows and exactly what she wants.

La Source (© *Martha Swope*)

Union Jack (© Martha Swope)

Other Dances, (right) with Suzanne Farrell (© Martha Swope)

Vienna Waltzes, (above) with Heather Watts (© Martha Swope)

When she returned to the company, after her five-year absence, she said to me in class, "My God, are you still here? I thought it would be the end of you when I left." Yes, she was kidding, but there was truth in her implication that when she had left I had had to progress in the company without the protective cover of her need for a partner.

She returned very changed. In her early years with Balanchine he had pampered her, made her look good, supplied her with what she needed. Displaying her in the many ways he saw her, he had created her style and manipulated it: from the ideal and dream woman Dulcinea in his *Don Quixote* to the prima ballerina assoluta of *Diamonds*, two kinds of female perfection, distant reflections, one of the other, but each essentially similar to the other.

A difficult adjustment time comes for dancers when the exhilaration and strength of early youth is over, when unlimited energy is not there all the time and the artist within must take control. Suzanne made that adjustment while she was away, and came back a stagewise artist, a very canny performer. She had developed a method of surviving as a dancer, and she had taken over for herself the protective, nurturing role that Balanchine had assumed for her in her early years. Nevertheless, her devotion to Balanchine is absolute, and Balanchine has been the reason she dances. Her goals have been to dance in Balanchine ballets.

Whenever I return to her, it is as if I had been away for a time, and to return to her is the most natural thing in the world. It is as if I'd been staying away in comfortable hotels, yet now I've come back to where I'm best known, where the landscape is familiar, and where I am most at ease. Neither of us has a difficult temperament, and we have never had a verbal fight. We have both been discouraged and disappointed with each other and we have had to turn our backs on each other at times, but these have been breaches that have been repaired easily.

She is a great ballerina, and I have respect for her. She is the ultimate version of a fine breed of dancer, the great Balanchine ballerina. She is the last of her kind in her frame of mind, in her way of looking at ballet and how she conceives her place. The new ones think of themselves as dancers, not as ballerinas. They are not concerned with images and do not have a sense of rare privilege. Suzanne Farrell has the great manner and dignity, something we name of the old world. She has the grand style.

Suzanne and I have danced together for so long that she has learned to trust me and to know that I will be there when she will need me, and this allows her to forget about me, and to just go about her dancing. It gives her even more freedom. Other dancers will need the security of knowing my presence all the time, and indeed it is the lively, active feel of the partner's presence that reassures them. All this changes from dancer to dancer, and it also depends on the dancer's present condition. A dancer will tell you what she wants, and she'll tell you when you aren't giving her what she wants. Ballerinas always bitch: you can't lift worth a damn; don't hold me there; touch me; don't touch me.

Years ago I was told by a ballerina after a raucous, badly timed performance to pull myself together and to learn a few things, to shape up. She was tired of my incompetence and nonsense. So I told her to shut up and to tell the company director if she didn't want to dance with me. She never complained again, and I actually treasure the memory of our performances. She would direct me through them right on stage: "Touch me higher, right on the tits. Come on, don't be afraid, they aren't going to bump into you 'cause there isn't much of them anyway."

There was another dancer who was less of a problem and less fun because she was so slight. She was too light, too like a feather. I didn't feel I was dancing with anything. The male partner needs to feel his partner's weight and opposition — it is the play of forces which gives a sense of drama. The audience needs to see dynamic interaction. (Suzanne's trust and her freedom to not worry about me *is* an interaction — it gives variety to the dancing, a way of measuring it out.) If nothing is there, then nothing happens, and all you see are two dancers wandering around the stage, not as if they seem to be wishing the other would go away, but as if they didn't know the other was there at all.

A dancer of the same weight and height as the slight one gave me a different problem. The weightlessness of the almost invisible one came from her *over*participation (helping with a jump in a lift), but this one just placed herself and let me do all the lifting, with no help at all. Dancing with this pint-sized ballerina was like dancing with a truck. A heavy dancer is a heavy dancer, but a big one can be as light for a partner as anyone else, if she dances light and with participation.

A dancer I admired, and for very different reasons from those I've given for other dancers, was Violette Verdy. I don't think I had realized before working with Violette how much I could admire a female dancer, and how much I could learn from one. All my models, instructors, and rivals had been male dancers, but from Violette I learned phrasing, timing, shaping. I also learned about partnering. I think she was so fine an instructor because she said early on in our working together that she could never tell me anything about partnering. She was complimenting me on my responsiveness to her needs, and she asked me questions about how I managed her. Her questions made me more aware; I watched her more carefully and respected her refinement. I saw how carefully thought out and intelligent her dancing was. The task as a partner then became not merely to anticipate her movement but to match her manner, to scale my dancing down to fit her precision so that we seemed to be coming from the same ballet world. I danced *with* her.

Unlike most of the dancers who were principals at the time I joined the company, Violette was not a Balanchine product. Before her association with Balanchine she had danced with Roland Petit's Ballets de Paris, with London Festival Ballet, and with Ballet Theatre. She was a self-made dancer, not one shaped by a choreographer, and she found her own, distinctive style by herself. That she made the right choices is evidence of her rare quickness and intelligence. It serves to make her an excellent teacher, for she has a ready sympathy for other dancers and for dance problems. With her culture, sensitivity and experience she was marked early to be a director of a company, and I think the world has yet to feel her real force.

Melissa Hayden was another self-made dancer, with an already-established reputation because of her work with Ballet Theatre, when she joined the NYCB. She did not have Violette's international experience, but she was as finely trained a dancer as I have known, and she was a blunt, forthright, clear and sensationally challenging partner.

My ideas of dance in America came from Jerome Robbins. *West Side Story* is one of my all-time favorite works, a masterwork I have loved each time I've seen it. I saw it first in Denmark, and last in the summer of 1981 in Monte Carlo. I always respond to it with feelings of discovery and wonder and I'm still flabbergasted and amazed every time I encounter it, for its emotional intensity, choreographic inventiveness, and brilliant staging. It remains an explosion of talent, fresh, new-born always, and it represents the period and aspects of America that first attracted me. It is a work with no inhibitions, where you feel the choreographer inventing the dance vocabulary. It seems to me that though Robbins is an acknowledged master in the pure balletic vocabulary, he is at his greatest when he has the freedom to bring in other movement, and when his genius for staging and drama and for downright showmanship is given free rein.

The company now performs two of his earliest works, *Fancy Free*, first made for ABT in 1944, and *Interplay*, a ballet that was first seen in a musical revue, *Concert Varieties*, in 1945. These have a craft and design that are distinctively Robbins. *Interplay* is really American kids conquering the classical vocabulary, taking it for their own and giving it jazz energy and romance, turning it into a game. It is a fresh-kid ballet. The cast is like a group of teenagers, dance teenagers, and they are from the period in which they were invented: you think of *hip* and *jivey* and *yeah* and *okay*. When I look at that ballet it becomes apparent that no one other than Jerry could have made this.

Working with Robbins can be maddening, for he is a difficult master — almost (but not absolutely) impossible to please, meticulous and exacting about the minutest detail. The first two roles made on me in the United States were by Jerry: in *In the Night* I partnered Violette Verdy in the second section, and a solo and a duet with Karin von Aroldingen in *The Goldberg Variations*.

The first *Goldberg* rehearsal for my solo was, well, mind-blowing. I trotted over to the Juilliard studio all excited because at last I had a major role in what was going to be a big, big work. When I got there I found Jerry, with the pianist, looking depressed and tired.

"Peter, this is the last thing in the world I want to do. Sorry about that. I'm just not in the mood. But I have to, I guess. To tell you the truth, there just isn't any inspiration in me today."

Obviously, *I* wasn't going to be able to change his depressed state. So I just stood there. What was I supposed to do? Tell him it was okay, pack up my bag and go?

He stretched out his arms and dropped his head, then flexed his wrists and bent his knees, the very picture of lack of inspiration. Suddenly aware of what he must look like, he said, "Say, let's start with this. This sort of looks good."

So that's just how my solo in *Goldberg* opened. But the making of the rest took the most out of me. No other choreographer had worked me over like that. Every movement, every bit of phrasing, every glance, the force of a touch, the width of a hand, everything was specifically named and demanded. I kept saying, "I don't get this," and he'd say, "You're getting it, you're getting it. It's looking good," and much of the time I couldn't tell the difference between when I was getting it and when I wasn't.

Because of his precise, detailed, airtight. instructions, I feel confined when I dance certain of his ballets, like *Afternoon of a Faun*. Every movement and emotion is built in. I think it is a work that suits best, and is more easily danced by, young dancers, who are less self-aware, who have fewer self-concepts about themselves as dancers.

Robbins shows this extraordinary intelligence in how his ballets are constructed. He understands how far to go and how far not to go. He knows when to start and what is exactly enough. His is a supreme theatrical sensibility, and he understands the American public.

For the Ravel festival, he made *In G Major* (originally titled *Concerto in G*) for Suzanne and myself, and that period of creation was a wonderful experience for me. Suzanne and I felt he wanted to make a beautiful *pas de deux*, and he constantly made clear how interested he was in us as dancers, and that he had no ideal notion of what this piece absolutely must be like. He asked us what we thought, and he used some of our ideas.

For a gala benefit performance in the spring of 1979, Baryshnikov, Jean-Pierre Frohlich and I did the sequence of solos from Jerry's *Fancy Free*, and the following season the full work was added to the repertory. The rehearsals nearly drove me out of my mind, for Jerry's way is to teach the material (the steps) and the interpretation at the same time, where I prefer to learn the material and then interpret (if it needs interpretation) once the material is second nature. Perhaps this was due to his knowing the ballet so well, and he had such an unalterable picture of how this role should be done that he was especially scrupulous. The problem was compounded because he loves to rehearse and I hate rehearsing. I'd touch someone on the back, and I'd be told no, the touch was too light and a bit high, but don't make it too heavy, and I'd touch again and be told no, like this, like this, couldn't I see the difference? I'd squint at the "like this" and guess maybe the third and fourth fingers were touching and the thumb was maybe spread out a little, and I'd try that. No, no, like this!

Robbins is a man of courage and impeccable artistic sense — it takes this to place his work next to Balanchine's. His glorious talent and gift is not like Balanchine's, but the comparison is insisted on by critics anyway, and I think Robbins becomes an even greater artist because he allows and appreciates this opportunity to work with the master. The world is his for the asking, and he has chosen to be with what he believes is the best.

His contribution to the company has been determining and crucial. Balanchine knew what more was needed, and he invited Robbins in. When Robbins took a long sabbatical Balanchine made him know he would be welcomed back whenever he was ready to return and given what he wanted.

Another company association, a very brief one, also contributed to dance history. One of the first ballets Mikhail Baryshnikov learned when he joined the Ballet Theatre after defecting from the Soviet Union in Toronto

Afternoon of a Faun, with Allegra Kent
(these pages and overleaf: © Martha Swope)

was Balanchine's *Theme and Variations*. We had met first in Leningrad, when the NYCB was touring Russia, and undiplomatically and presumptuously, I told him the best thing he could do would be to come to the United States and dance with us — leave his native country, just as I had done. He laughed me off, and waved me away.

A friend had filmed for me in Russia Baryshnikov doing the *Don Quixote Pas de Deux*, and I watched it over and over, full of admiration and full of envy. I wanted to be the best dancer in the world, and there on the screen before me was someone better than I was. I realized that for the past few years I had been asleep, for I hadn't been forcing or pushing myself. The more I watched the film, the more convinced I was that there wasn't anything he was doing that I couldn't do if I worked at it. Even though he was in the Soviet Union, and I was in the United States, the fact that he existed set a standard. There was this dancer far superior, far superior . . .

I could see even then that he was the only dancer who didn't make you focus on the trick itself, for he managed to incorporate the trick into the role. This ability came from his sense of style, from his stage sense. He was always tasteful, never tacky, and this abetted his phenomenal physical ability.

When the news came of his defection, I thought now he would come to us, and I kept on insisting how good this would be for him when we next saw each other. His success when he did defect and come to the United States was of the kind given to movie celebrities, and with this, there grew a gulf between what I was advising, being a member of a company, and what has happened to him, becoming a world superstar.

But Misha learned more Balanchine roles, while Balanchine coolly continued to profess that he had no idea what his dancing was like for he had never seen him.

Baryshnikov felt uneasy with his success, and yearned for the kind of structure that he had had as a member of the Kirov. He had said he had come to the West to extend the range of his dancing, to grow as an artist, and it was true. In the United States alone, he grabbed the chance to work with Twyla Tharp, Paul Taylor, Eliot Feld, Alvin Ailey, and he knew there was one more, the ultimate, and one day he asked me how to approach Balanchine. I told him what had been told me: that you have to make clear you are willing to be a company member, willing to place yourself in its ranks and serve its needs. No name above the title, no star stuff.

I have been told that Balanchine first saw Misha dance when the film *The Turning Point* was screened for him, and his reaction was: not bad, a good dancer. A dinner was arranged for just the two of them. As Balanchine described it: "We had appetizers, and had vodka and beer. Misha became very impulsive, and I said, well, if he'd like, that's fine, so we skipped the main course and toasted many people with more vodka, and we were both happy to have the question out of the way." In fact, Balanchine was very enthusiastic, full of plans, telling everyone Misha was a wonderful dancer who could do everything.

The news came as a sensation, the meeting of this great choreographer and this great dancer — it was the kind of match that one dreamed of but thought would never happen in "real life." Speculations began about what Misha would dance and with whom, if Balanchine would make new works for him, if this would last, if Baryshnikov could give up the celebrity. Would we never see him again in *Giselle* or *Sleeping Beauty*? I was overjoyed that we would be working together, for he is a close friend, and I felt justified because I had been urging this for years.

Baryshnikov can adapt to any style and understand it within minutes. It is uncanny to me, this gift of immediate sympathy and comprehension. I had always thought that I had the same ability and that inherently I have a great range until I met Misha. He was faster at adapting to a new dance style, and he did it more easily and with less ideological obstacles than I bring. I had to confess to myself that this dancer was given more talent than I was — and though close friends would warn me not to say it, I have to say that I do have a lot of talent.

From his parents he got the equipment. He inherited the parts of a body that are good for a dancer. And he happened to be born in the right place at the right time. He had the best training available, and around him were those who knew what to do with his talent and gift. Also, from the start, he had an absolutely perfect, healthy attitude toward dancing, and with that attitude he wasn't going to muck up his life. He doesn't have a mad obsession for dancing, although in itself that obsession isn't necessarily destructive — it just opens you to trouble. He isn't maniacally disciplined; possibly his zest for the variety of existence, with his openness to all experience, participates in making him a great dancer.

This is something one sees in his dancing: chance-taking, guts, energy, and that intense commitment that is a love of life, a joy that is selfless. He makes the joy of dancing vivid, makes clear that he is having a fabulous time doing what he is doing. And with it all, he has tremendous professionalism. Just once I saw him nervous, the first time I saw him do *Theme and Variations* with Ballet Theatre at the Metropolitan Opera House, and I thought how attractive that was, for this great, great dancer to be showing his responsibility to his work.

When he was with the NYCB he didn't behave in any way like a superstar, and the company liked him immediately. He showed his vulnerability, and an underlying insecurity (such insecurity serves to goad a dancer; without that, you'd be complacent and dead). His first roles were Villella signature pieces: *Rubies, Tarantella, Prodigal Son*. Villella coached him some, but Balanchine wanted no imitative performances and pushed Misha to do these roles his own way, and Misha tried other pieces: Melancholic in *The Four Temperaments*, *Orpheus*, *Stars and Stripes*, *Steadfast Tin Soldier*, *Donizetti Variations*.

Balanchine was recovering from an illness and this curtailed his activities, so he couldn't make new pieces, but he revived *Prodigal Son*, *Apollo* (in a shortened version), *La Sonnambula* with Misha especially in mind. Robbins made *Opus 19/The Dreamer* for Misha, and the last movement, "Fall," to *The Four Seasons* (to Verdi's ballet music from *I Vespri Siciliani*). Of the last there were two versions, one for Misha and Patricia McBride, and the other for Suzanne Farrell and me.

117

Baryshnikov's time with the NYCB was a marvelous experiment, and there was excitement and enlightenment for the audience and for his fellow dancers in watching how this dance genius approached and tried to encompass these roles. His efforts had nothing to do with good or bad, or "less good" and "better than" — the real stuff of a dancer's art has nothing to do with this kind of judgment. Every performance, fully realized, or not there at all, or totally misconceived, I thought a triumph because of his valiant commitment to his work, a commitment that was beautiful and sometimes painful to witness.

There were problems. Balanchine let him do everything, assigned him everything. It was a crash course and would have been daunting for a younger dancer. Baryshnikov had entered later in his career than was usual for new members of the company, and he suffered the kinds of entrance problems I suffered, and that were suffered also by Erik Bruhn, Peter Schaufuss, Jean-Pierre Bonnefous, Adam Lüders, Ib Andersen, Helgi Tomasson, all of us trained elsewhere and where there wasn't such constant and so big a repertory. All of us sustained flare-ups of tendinitis, a common ailment of male dancers with the NYCB but which goes away after a year when your strength in those areas that Balanchine technique and choreography demand has been developed.

Baryshnimov feared he was losing some of his technical mastery, and there was the constant problem of conquering a repertory that every dancer around him tossed off. He would worry that he wasn't as good as so many others in the same role. He wanted to know he was showing his supremacy, not in some egotistic, self-promoting way, but he wanted to see for himself and the audience to know his special contribution. He was especially brilliant in the Costermonger *pas de deux* as the Pearly King in *Union Jack*, achingly funny. And he just couldn't understand what was so good about his performance. It seemed so slight a piece.

Another problem: a partner. Finding a girl both to complement and match has been always a question. Gelsey Kirkland was wonderful with him when he was with ABT, but temperament, perhaps company politics and

The Four Seasons, with Suzanne Farrell (© Martha Swope)

Scotch Symphony, with Suzanne Farrell (left: © Martha Swope; right: © Steven Caras)

*Fancy Free, (above) with Stephanie Saland;
(below) with Mikhail Baryshnikov (above and right:
© Martha Swope; below: © Steven Caras)*

Robert Schumann's "Davidsbündlertänze," with Heather Watts (© Martha Swope)

Mozartiana (© Steven Caras)

ambitions made them an uneasy match. Ironically, she had left the NYCB some years before for the very reason of being free to dance with Misha.

Patricia McBride, who had been Villella's greatest partner and the co-beneficiary of such Balanchine ballets as *Rubies, Harlequinade, Tarantella* — and Balanchine had made for her the great "Fascinatin' Rhythm" solo and "The Man I Love" *pas de deux* in *Who Cares?* — was Misha's most frequent partner. Though both brought effort and respect to the team, the combination lacked magic. What I feel was missing was either an identical perspective that would have made them conform to each other, or contrasting styles that would have given the pair a complementary sharpness, like the match of Fonteyn and Nureyev.

McBride and Misha are both breathtaking technicians, elegant performers, and one felt their admiration and giving, but one couldn't feel or be able to imagine the possibility of a deep artistic rapport. It might have happened if Misha had stayed a while longer, for Pat was imbued with the style, and Misha was working to define it and make it absolutely his own; possibly, when he had caught up, it would all have fit.

Misha stayed for two years, and I think of it as a glorious period. Then he was offered the directorship of American Ballet Theatre, and he accepted with Balanchine's encouragement and aid. Balanchine gave Misha *Prodigal Son* and *La Sonnambula*, ballets that Misha excelled in for us and that Misha presented in exciting productions with ABT dancers. Their firm friendship continues. Misha had gotten what he wanted: he had had his experience.

For me, it was a challenge and education to have this exemplar of great dancing always around, and to have my friend so close. We are different dancers, with different ambitions, and that makes our friendship easier. There are even days I miss Misha's imitations of me in class, jaw jutting out, stern, cool. But I don't think he's missing my imitations of his single *pirouettes*, or missing what he left behind.

CHAPTER FOUR

Thoughts on Dance

*E*ven *before* I began working with Balanchine, I already had decided opinions about dancing, of what was right and what false, what good and what hideous. I found with Balanchine the confirmation and demonstration of an attitude and approach that made sense to me. It is an attitude shared, I believe, by Stanley Williams; it is an approach to dancing that I think commonsensical, down to earth.

It amounts to a philosophy of dance, if you will, and I want that philosophy to show in my dancing — in the way I perform, and in the dances that I make. It is a value system that most narrowly concerns classical ballet, but it is *classical* ballet and the modern forms of classical ballet that I have devoted myself to.

What I found in Balanchine was a master who could make clear what it was I was striving for, who could make clear how to realize what ballet could and should be. It includes a way of dancing that demands directness and clarity and simplicity. It is a strong belief in the power of dancing in and of itself.

In dance, the craftsman-dancer is the one who strives to do the steps accurately, to dance the part so that all its potential is shown, to do justice to all the technical challenges, all the relationships — of shape, of design, of steps to the music. The perfect way of dancing, and that perfecting of dancing, tells you it is a craft. And before you impose or inject something of your own, you have to have mastered that craft.

I work for perfection, and though I am bound to be frustrated this unattainable goal serves to keep me striving, anxious to fulfill, anxious to keep moving, always fighting my own impatience. When, on stage, I am showing the audience what I can do, what I have to offer, what it is that I do best, and when through my dancing I am saying this is me at my best, I am at my happiest.

I've always had a great dislike for overexpressive dancers. I hate people who overreact and who interpret when there isn't a need for any interpretation. Just about the worst sin I could commit (on stage) would be to dance poorly and disguise it by spreading my soul all over the stage, emoting and suffering and yearning, or being thrillingly happy. I'd like to crack over the head dancers who do that. Similarly, I'm irritated by dancers who point out to you what lovely feet they have, and how beautifully they move their arms, who beam smiles and winks into the audience to show you what great guys they are. The feeling must be part of the dancing itself, the whole body must be thought of as expressive and you can't smudge dancing with mime and pour syrup all over it to make it palatable.

Coating dance with syrup (and/or sex) is a trick some choreographers use to cover their lack of a firm ability to use dance vocabulary — they don't know their stuff. Dancers use these same tricks when they feel insecure, and when they know the choreography is insipid and repetitious. Some choreographers use certain dancers over and over just for the dancer's ability to hide the absence of choreographic substance by acting and emphasizing and carrying on. This way of dancing and choreographing is a fraud, and I think the astute members of the audience feel the fakery right away.

The directness and simplicity of approach that I like has led me to be accused of undercoaching the ballets I have choreographed — that is, not telling the dancers enough — and also of underrehearsing the ballets I dance. But I don't want to smooth away energy and impulsiveness, and I want to leave space for the dancer to fill in with his or her own distinctiveness.

This accounts in large part for my not liking to rehearse generally. Once I've learned a role and have danced it often, I don't like to run through it all full out just before a performance. Such thorough rehearsing plus a performance gives me the sense of having done the ballet twice in a row, and it will have been the performance in front of the audience that suffered for lacking spontaneity. Needless to say, you need to know what you are doing — in order not to do it.

In the New York City Ballet, the ratio of rehearsal time to performance is much smaller than with other companies, and that is because we perform so often and because of the size of our repertory, and some of our critics say that the repertory looks underrehearsed too much of the time. As our season progresses, ballets that were scheduled to enter the repertory late are dropped because of the lack of rehearsal time. The number of ballets in our repertory is extraordinarily high because we need the variety to keep our subscription audiences happy. They don't want to see the same ballets season after season.

There are times when the performance itself could be called justly a rehearsal. There is the rehearsal right on the stage, for the whole world to see. But for an alert and involved audience this can prove to be the occasion for insight into what makes a dancer special, and how dance roles are shaped, developed and defined. Dancers are always growing and changing — they take class every day not only to maintain their best physical condition but to refine their skills — just so every performance can be a further defining and a further honing of a role. Perhaps this is not an ideal situation, but it is a present and probably inescapable reality.

Great, perfect performances are rare and unpredictable. It is a matter of luck for the dancers and for the audience. What you find in the less-than-perfect performances I am talking about is the dancer in the process of discovering how best to perform a role, and when you see the dancer next in that same part you'll find what the dancer has learned and what aspect is being developed. As in no other performing art, the spectator is made a participant. This is among the reasons for attending frequently, and to observe that growth and change is what rivets the attention and caring of an audience to a dancer.

Great dancers do not repeat their performances: their *Giselle* or *Theme and Variations*, their Odette or their *Push Comes to Shove*, will be different each time they dance it. There is no final and decided performance of a role. Dancing happens, dancing is always in the present. When a dancer can no longer find anything to challenge and explore in a role, then he should relinquish it. If you do a role too often it can come to feel old hat and you risk losing the sense of the role's shape. There are certain roles that I have wanted to take a rest from for a season or two for just this reason. I had to forget them slightly so that my next performance was a renewed experience.

Until fairly recently, I never liked class, yet I was always a class dancer. I was terrific in class and for some reason I felt my onstage dancing was less free and less exciting — perhaps it was the pressure of an audience that was slightly inhibiting. As I said before, my reason for not liking to rehearse was that if I "did it" in rehearsal, I'd be less likely to do it on stage. There has been the complaint about my dancing that I seemed too cool and glacial, distant emotionally, overly meticulous. Some felt that my dancing displayed an unwillingness to project any personality, and there was the implied criticism, I thought, that I didn't have enough of a personality.

The "personality" phenomenon became a confusing issue to me. When I first came to the United States, I was involved with people who talked a lot about personality and it was always the outrageous, the uninhibited who were characterized as having personality. Just because you were wild and inconsistent, you seemed to demonstrate a "fabulous personality." Personality meant more than that to me. It had to do with being aware of yourself, having your own opinions which you were secure enough about that you didn't have to advertise yourself.

When I was younger I felt uncomfortable before an audience, and frankly this hasn't changed much! For one thing, I was physically larger than other dancers when I began. Now dancers seem a race of giants, and when I was in Denmark recently, I felt dwarfed by some of the younger dancers. All of them were much bigger than I was. But since I was physically big, my dancing read large — I made a clear impression — and early on I understood that my whole body must be active and full, just because I was so big. Some tall and broad dancers look so dead on stage because they are trying to dance as if, literally, they weren't all there.

A talent I've always had is of being a fast learner — I've learned whole ballets in one day — but quick learning has a consequence: you forget quickly; at least, I do. A dancer's ability to learn choreography almost immediately comes from years of training, and from the logic of movement. In learning music you don't necessarily learn note for note, you learn the musical shape, and so it goes in dance. The music is the clue for what happens next, but modern choreographers have shown that dance logic can be separated from the music. The muscles, the body, learn ways to move. A dancer gets lost when he falls out of sequence.

I was a good turner, and I had a good jump — height wasn't emphasized in my training, but timing and quality were, and we were called upon to find that happy medium which allowed a jump of sufficient height coupled with a soft landing. I knew I was considered good at partnering, and that this commanded respect, if not always from the audience then at least from other dancers and from company directors. Although I'm not totally sympathetic when I see young boys wincing when all that seems required of them is to be a *porteur*, to carry and support and show off the girl, I do understand their feelings. But I have no tolerance and no sympathy at all when they do it grudgingly and badly: after all, they are dancers and partnering is certainly as important as dancing itself.

Partnering came naturally to me, and I suppose I had a talent for it. I understood the challenge of it immediately, and what I liked was the play between the man and woman. There was pride in being responsible for displaying the girl, in being responsible for how she was presented, showing what she could do. Also, there was a relief, and still is, in shifting off the concentration from myself. The girl was the first priority.

I knew something else: the girl made me look good, for making the girl look her best reflects back on the boy, and both in contrast and relation the boy will gain — if he is aware of the effect, and lucky in his partners. It has to be this mutual reflection that makes a working partnership. The girls are wondering always what the boy can do for her; when in addition they know what they can do for the boy, then a rapport begins that makes possible what the audience loves: a wonderful partnership.

While I think it is the vicarious romance of a dance partnership that an audience likes, the public is less appreciative of the technical difficulties of partnering than of solo dancing because they have not been introduced to its refinements. What they see is a boy lifting the girl, throwing her and catching her, carrying her around the stage, keeping a firm hand on her waist even when she seems to be trying to kick him in the face, and getting out of her way when she starts whipping out turns. This absence of appreciation might be caused by that attitude of male dancers which indicates to an audience: "All I have to do is stand around while she's being great, and get behind her so she doesn't flop over, and frankly I'm not doing anything but keeping an eye out for her. And at the same time I'm taking a lot of abuse for not holding her enough or for holding her too much." (Ballerinas reserve their worst language for their partners. And another thing I'd like to get off my chest: ballerinas come in all sizes and shapes. Some are nice, some are not so nice. But they all possess in common those elements necessary to make a ballerina: they are all tough, merciless, self-centered, narrow-minded, and without awareness of and interest in the needs of her male counterpart. When a ballerina looks in the rehearsal hall mirror she only sees herself; and when her partner looks in the same mirror he sees not himself but only her. Of course, the obvious reason is that she's always standing in front of him!)

From my first class, I was aware that partnering was an active act. It was immediately clear how important my function in this was: it concerned how I lifted her, how I presented her, how I promenaded her. What you learn first in *adagio* class is to promenade with the girl, who is on point in attitude, then to support her in arabesque, and in turns. My first *adagio* class teacher, Frank Schaufuss, taught me that though a promenade was simply a walk, to have an effect it needs a slight resistance, a gentle force and tension. The girl resists the boy so that he sets her into place; there must be a constant play of yielding and resisting.

I discovered for myself methods of partnering, certain tricks, if you will, by applying common sense. One thing I found in the process of dancing was how to release and relax the hands, paring down their use to the absolute essential for what you need for control, without the public being aware of how I was manipulating the girl. For instance, instead of using my full hand to direct her promenade, by clasping her hand in a full grasp, I extend my index finger to her pulse and manipulate with that. Therefore, the hand doesn't twist, it holds firm, and the finger is working on the underside, out of sight of the audience.

After supported arabesques, you learn to hold a girl in *pas de bourrées*, then to support her *pirouettes*. After that, to stop her turns, so they come to a graceful conclusion, and then finally you learn to lift her.

These first lifts are in combination with her jumping, and only when the boys have strength do they do lifts without the aid of the girl's jumping at the same time. Boys do push-ups and work out with weights to increase their strength. But the male dancer can never lift the girl from just the use of a strong back and arms. What I had to learn was to lift with my thighs, to involve my whole body in the lift. Force upward in dance begins with the *plié*, that bend of the knees that is preliminary to the spring upward, and so with a lift: it begins with a slight bend and then a push up with the whole body.

It was from Balanchine that I learned the aesthetics of good partnering, and he reshaped a lot of what I had been doing. This began with his stressing the distance the man places between himself and the woman. He kept insisting we make room between ourselves. When a girl is doing unsupported work, don't just stand right behind her preparing for her next need of you — or worse, keep your hands on her waist — just get out of the way! When she is ready to start her turns, then move in to support her.

Balanchine is always working to keep the images clear, to keep the picture in focus all the time. For instance, when the girl is running across the stage to end in a *piqué arabesque*, supported, then the boy and girl do not run at the same time. First we see her go, then he goes and he will only catch up with her when she does *piqué arabesque*.

The point is to show the woman in isolation — to display her, to allow her to be free, and then to make clear that you are showing this woman in her fullest capabilities. You are there to make her realize her potential. No remark of Balanchine's has been so widely quoted and so badly misunderstood as the aforementioned "Ballet is woman." This is not meant to diminish the importance of male dancers, but it is the expression of relationship of what the man and the woman state together, and how the man perceives and pays honor. It is a courtly and romantic notion, but it does not exclude men — or absolve them of responsibility.

One famous ballerina complained once that though I was a fantastically secure partner — she was sweetening the criticism to come — my style was incorrect aesthetically for the nineteenth-century classics. (Incidentally, this is a common correction from Russian dancers also about non-Russian dancers.) Not only was my style incorrect, it was inappropriate. I shouldn't be leaving her alone so much, I should be hovering and solicitous and always there and always concerned. I told her that I wanted her to look as if she was doing everything herself, that indeed I wanted to keep my distance, and to make my presence known only when it had to be. Gentlemanly discretion is a component of a good partnership.

There is a distinction to be made between what is academic and what is classical. This reverence for the idea of a re-creation of what the nine-teenth-century style was actually like is an academic and maybe interesting effort, but it is ridiculous for actual practice, and useless as a theatrical objective when it comes to the practical necessities of dancing, how we are physically different, what theater design is like, for how dancers are trained today, for the times we live in.

I don't really understand this need for precise re-creation — with all respect to Petipa and Bournonville and the other old masters, this dancing in what is considered to be the correct old style all looks strained and irrelevant, and also it often looks wrong. Ballet just couldn't have been so silly. Dances re-created from notation alone look spiritless and without point. Add to this some need to act out manners and styles of a different era, and dance becomes a real trial to watch. To return to the way the ballet was originally performed and intended to be performed would require the audience to adopt the mentality of a previous era, to see with the eyes

Bournonville Divertissements, with Suzanne Farrell (© Martha Swope)

Bournonville Divertissements, with Suzanne Farrell
(© Martha Swope)

Bournonville Divertissements, with Merrill Ashley
(left top: © Carolyn George; left bottom: © Costas;
right: © Martha Swope)

Tzigane, with Suzanne Farrell (left, and right bottom: © Martha Swope; right top: © Steven Caras)

Tchaikovsky Pas de Deux, (below) with Merrill Ashley (above:
© Steven Caras; below: © Martha Swope)

La Sylphide (© Linda Vartoogian)

Chaconne, (right) with Suzanne Farrell (left: © Steven Caras; right: © Martha Swope)

Chaconne (© Costas)

of a different period, and to banish all the lighting and technical facilities of a theater. It could well be that we have lost the lavish stagecraft and design genius of the nineteenth century, and that in that way, today's theater is simply inferior. Theatrical spectacle is merely suggested in today's productions.

The vitality and force of classical dance is maintained by its thorough relation to the present. The effort is to make classical ballet come alive, not through documentary re-creations alone, but through extensions of the language, to always feel its lively possibilities. We dance in the present and in a way, thank God, we don't know how we will dance in the future. Of course, the past has significance for me, but no more importance for me in the present than the future.

Knowing how hard it is to achieve anything in this profession, and knowing how much luck in addition to thousands of other elements goes into becoming a successful dancer, I object strenuously when I hear other dancers or teachers classify dancers as types (this is, of course, an introduction to doing just that), and I feel rebellious when I read a critic's categorizations. The complicated business of describing a dancer has been simplified to an insulting tag. Nonetheless, I am always grouping dancers in my own special categories, which involve the way I think about and see dancers, not "rating" them on a scale of excellence. I don't intend these groupings as an aid to defining dancers but to offer a way one dancer perceives his co-workers.

My first group consists of those who strike me as "born" to dance, who have an innate impulse and seem to have been fated to be nothing else but dancers. There are numerous dancers who fit this category (and the two other categories I'll name), but the most obvious who come to mind in the first group are Patricia McBride and Mikhail Baryshnikov.

Then there are those dancers whose ability and facility are the first of their qualities to appear when I think of them, and their natural ability is beyond what any training can give. Suzanne Farrell qualifies as the prime example here.

My third group I call "made" dancers, craftsmen, workers. These are dancers who seem to create themselves as dancers, who *will* themselves to be dancers, and I think here of Merrill Ashley, Gelsey Kirkland, and Rudolph Nureyev. Not that these dancers or the above-mentioned have only the exclusive feature of their group, but these qualities are the ones that their dancing brings to mind consistently and that I find most distinctive. Clearly, the dancers who exhibit all three qualities over one specific one are rare, but nevertheless they exist.

I can think of countless other examples, for all the dancers who interest me fit into one of these categories. What fascinates me is that nature provides the basic elements of these categories: talent, physicality, character.

A great dancer has to have a balanced and healthy attitude to dancing, for dancing makes very unique emotional demands. Because they lacked this perspective, thousands of talented dancers who could have been great didn't fulfill their promise, and then there are those with lesser talents who have succeeded just because their attitude has been more focused, because they have known how to avoid the traps of dance ambitions. So many dancers fail because of circumstances: they have not been in the right place at the right time, or they have not been brave and sought out opportunities. Perhaps through no fault of their own, they have no control over their careers. Or they drive themselves in the wrong ways, they ignore what are their best opportunities, they become trapped in envy of other dancers, become bitter and dispirited when they feel they have been overlooked by teachers and ballet masters. The popular view is that the harder you work, the better dancer you are, but that is not necessarily so. These are the dancers who go from class to class, from teacher to teacher, searching for the one with the magic formula, and who constantly model themselves after celebrated dancers. The mistake these determined, consumed, voracious dancers are making is that they are not trying to find *their* way. They are not trusting themselves and their personal qualities.

These are the devils, temptations, and traps dancers have to avoid, and as I name them you can see these are not merely worldly traps, which are easier to be on guard against, but gnawing thoughts and doubts and worries that drive dancers crazy. Dancers need more than willfulness and dedication. They must know what to try for and what not to, and they must know something of proportion, for they must maintain some healthy relation with the rest of the world.

CHAPTER FIVE

Company Existence

The New York City Ballet alternates its seasons with the New York City Opera at the New York State Theater, both companies having moved there in the mid-sixties from the City Center Theatre on Fifty-fifth Street. They are parts of the performing-arts community called Lincoln Center. Opposite the State Theater, across the rectangular plaza, is Avery Fisher Hall, once known as Philharmonic Hall, and between them is the Metropolitan Opera House. In the spring when the opera season ends, the American Ballet Theatre appears at the Met and during the summer the Met houses foreign dance companies.

The block to the north of this complex is occupied by the Juilliard School. Juilliard has its own theater, the site of performances by its opera, dramatic, and music divisions. The school has its own dance division, but a section of the third floor is rented to the most influential dance academy in the United States, the School of American Ballet (SAB).

SAB was established in 1934 by George Balanchine and Lincoln Kirstein as a seedbed for American classical dance, for they knew that ballet could flourish in the United States only if early training began in a coherent, structured manner. From the students trained at the school would come the base of a company. Today a necessary route for those who want to be in the NYCB is attendance at this school; there are only a few company members who have not attended SAB, and in recent years, as far as I can remember, these few have all been boys.

The SAB entrance age is eight or nine; those who enter later attend an accelerated beginning class. SAB teachers and directors are sent on regular scouting trips across the country to find worthy talent, and gifted students in other cities are invited to attend summer classes, with the possibility (but not the probability) of later acceptance to the full school program. Scholarships are available.

Unlike the Royal Danish School, academic subjects are not included in the program, and a student has a serious choice to make at fourteen, because SAB classes are scheduled for early afternoon for that age group, and therefore conflict with classes at regular academic schools. Continuing students then have to attend a private school with flexible hours, or the Professional Children's School. Therefore, professional decisions must be made by dance students at a very young age, and even beginners are involved almost immediately in that process of selection, election, and weeding that never ends for a professional dancer. Each year brings increased physical demands, and further demands of time and concentration, and the regimen limits the range of a social life. Usually, by necessity and unalterable circumstance, dance students know only other dance students or those involved in the arts.

Even from the start of the education of any SAB student there is a clear goal — a dream first, then an alternative, then a possibility, then the only thing worth living for: to be a member of the New York City Ballet. By virtue of that ambition you are in competition with the others in your class. That charged atmosphere cannot be avoided, and its pressure can be the reason for leaving dance ambition behind altogether.

Advanced students take at the least ten classes a week, with older boys' class from 12:30 to 2, and another evening class from 5:30 to 7, and between those there are supported *adagio* classes, from 2:30 to 4. The girls have an *adagio* class, a variations class, *pointe* class, workshop class. And then for the advanced students there are also daily preparations for the spring workshop performance.

Mothers accompany their youngsters to class but have to stay outside and wait for them in the hallways or downstairs. The older students carry their textbooks with them and study in the breaks. Some who have moved to New York to study at SAB board in school-approved quarters, and some of the older ones take apartments together.

With all this there is no guarantee that anyone will be accepted into the New York City Ballet — or any other company, though of course the school is visited regularly, and raided regularly, by directors of companies from all over the world.

I have worked with the students of the school as a teacher and as a choreographer, and I have learned that one can tell early who is going to try for it, and who isn't. You have to be a fighter, and that battle is first with yourself, but it has to be also with negligent teachers, parents who worry you won't have a normal life, and those who tell you you have no talent.

Dance students are less sophisticated and perhaps more naive than their contemporaries, and also they seem to me kinder because they learn about pain much earlier, and their lives are built on effort. They are more compassionate because they live always in community; acuter and sharper because class forces intellectual agility; more beautiful because that is what their art requires; better mannered because manners and attention are asked of them hour upon hour every day. They are less corruptible and jaded, for though their craft requires self-concentration and self-protection, it also serves a vision beyond individual personalities, and these students know they can serve this vision for only a part of their lives.

Compared to the kids I knew in Denmark, students here move more, are more expressive and energetic. In Denmark they seemed more restricted, confined, and perhaps the bigness of this country accounts for that largeness in moving that I see here. The problem in America is to contain the kids' energy and to shape it. Students here have fewer preconceived notions of themselves as dancers, and they have an inexhaustible willingness to engage themselves fully.

This country lacks any real sense of ballet tradition, but I think that in part this is a plus, for the students are so moldable, have fewer inherited obstacles and preconceptions. The public here is like its dancers: uninhibited, excited, raw, with nothing to hide, with a craziness to give.

I am unusual in that I have never been an insecure dancer, but insecurity is the fate of most. Concern over being asked to join the company is only the first in a series of lifelong dance worries. Once in the company, and you usually enter as a corps member, you worry about whether you are going to be cast, and then when you *are* cast you wonder if your talents have been misunderstood and if this role is really right for you, or if you are capable of doing it and whether you will ever get any more roles. And you are always fighting the sense that no one is watching you or caring about you, in class and on stage. You worry about whether you can hold on to the roles you do have, and when you should just give the whole thing up (and do what? you don't know anything else!) because you've accomplished everything that you can accomplish and it's just going to be downhill from now on.

How can you call attention to yourself? By attending company class every day, by taking more classes, by watching all rehearsals, even those you haven't been called for? By smiling at the choreographers? By being friendly with the "right" people? By not being friendly with the "wrong" people? And what the hell does this have to do with dancing, dancers ask themselves, and why am I driving myself crazy about all this nonsense?

Will you ever make it to soloist ranks? Is there anyone to ask? And if you do ask, won't whoever it is tell you that you are a very limited dancer? Or tell you to be patient? And you don't want to hear either of these things. You'll resent those who are promoted over you, and who have less talent but are more aggressive, and those foreigners, like all those blank blond Danes they drag over — who needs them?

Then you are made a principal, and you wonder when you'll be given the roles that those other dancers look so terrible in and have clung to for too many years. Is the audience liking you, and how are they supposed to figure out who you are? Do the critics like you, and why are you ranked with dancers who are terrible? Then, why is *he* learning *your* role? Who is learning your role by shadowing you in the rehearsal room? Should you ask for a role, or will the act of asking assure that you'll never get it? Having achieved this principal status, what more should you do? Try for guest appearances? Make more money?

And the biggest worry of them all: Will Mr. B. make a ballet for me?

Constant through all this is a fear of physical injury. Such injuries can be very severe, but even the slightest ache sets off dread and terror in you for what it might indicate. I've sometimes thought that, to some extent, dancers determine their own injuries. Unless you have a chronic injury, you can prevent the little, minor ones from flaring up into something major. The more experienced you become, the more you learn to protect yourself and you protect yourself by knowing how your body works. Simply, a lot of injuries occur when dancers are careless. There are warning pains for certain injuries and either you take the warning or the consequence. On the other hand, dancers always ache. It's part of the game. Nureyev said to me, "If I don't ache and pain, I don't know I'm alive." This causes some dancers to become compulsive: they can't live without their masseur, their chiropractors, physical therapists, orthopedist, and special exercise studio. My chiropractor has on more than one occasion put me back on my feet.

This is an art all about control, and finally, with its risks, worries and dangers, you can't control it at all.

In the Spring 1981 season there were listed in the company roster 69 corps (43 girls and 26 boys), 12 soloists, and 18 principals. For the same period American Ballet Theatre had 55 corps, 25 soloists, and 13 principals; and Britain's Royal Ballet had 24 principal dancers, 12 "solo artists," 14 "coryphees," and 28 "artists." (Not all dancers listed are currently performing, and some might have as few as one or two roles.) Each rank has its separate problems and place in the company, resulting in a "rank" frame of mind. This is due to the kinds of work required of that rank (rehearsal, technical) and the sense of importance, both self-importance and outside attention.

Our New York seasons are long, and as a consequence we do not tour as frequently as other American companies. The fall season runs from mid-November to the end of February, the spring season goes from mid-April through June, and then we spend the month of July performing in Saratoga in upstate New York. This full schedule leaves little for much outside guesting or "gigs" (one-night, small-group appearances), and the NYCB had little national exposure until the series of PBS *Dance in America* television programs which featured the choreography of George Balanchine, and a *Live from Lincoln Center* performance of *Coppélia*. In recent years the company has appeared in Europe, with notable engagements in London, Paris, Copenhagen, Moscow, Berlin. But it remains a company with great prestige and, compared with companies of equal stature, less celebrity.

The company has a no-star policy and its repertory of ballets is not star oriented either. By and large the repertory is dancer-proof, and though major roles "belong" to certain dancers for a long stretch of time, especially if they were created on these dancers, the audience does not come especially to see a certain dancer do some ballet (except for devoted company watchers) in the way Ballet Theatre audiences come to see Natalia Makarova or Cynthia Gregory do *Giselle*.

The NYCB does not dance the nineteenth-century classic repertory, except for *Nutcracker*, *Coppélia* and a one-act version of *Swan Lake*. Our repertory consists of ballets by George Balanchine and Jerome Robbins, with some ballets by Jacques d'Amboise, John Taras and me. A NYCB dancer has to be subservient to the ballets and to Ballet. There are dancers whose talents are not best shown in this repertory, and there are dancers whose ambitions are not served by this stress on company above all.

Mr. Balanchine has been notorious for disliking dance prima donnas and the heady atmosphere they create. These are dancers who ordinarily think only of themselves, who have inflated notions of themselves, and who would have a hard time adjusting to our way of working, to the groundwork our performances are based on. He prefers dancers he has worked with over the years, dancers who have willingly and happily placed themselves at the disposal of his dance aesthetic.

Each season, two or three new ballets are announced. Given the problems of economics and time, what is planned and hoped for doesn't always happen, so not all of the new ballets appear. Sometimes, on the other hand, a work is unexpectedly ready, and "goes." The artistic control is absolutely and exclusively Balanchine's (though he will yield it on occasion), and this includes selection of dancers, their rankings, who will choreograph and how the ballets will be set and costumed.

The administrative function — concerned with negotiating contracts, managing the house, fund raising, subscription administration, living within a budget — is separate from the artistic one, but it is committed to serving Balanchine's ideals. Lincoln Kirstein is the General Director and he oversees the relation of the administrative, headed by Betty Cage, and artistic sections.

The company's orchestra occupies a position more important than in most ballet companies because of Balanchine's high musical standards, and its importance was made prominent especially during the company's Stravinsky, Ravel and Tchaikovsky festivals. The orchestra contract is negotiated with the musicians' union, and the dancers too have formed a union. Contract negotiations are not simple — the company has suffered both strikes and the threat of strikes of all sorts. But it is my guess that NYCB dancers have the best contract in America for a dance company. Since we are the best, we want the best.

Like the audiences for the Met and the New York Philharmonic, the NYCB audience is mostly subscription. This is an audience that picks favorites and makes clear its demands to the management by writing in requests for revivals, demanding that certain ballets be dropped, asking why their favorite dancers aren't given more roles, threatening to cancel their subscriptions if their requests aren't met. There is something small-town about it all — the intimacy of the way in which the company operates and the company's relation to its audience. The loftiness of the NYCB is in its achievement and its ideals, but it is not an august, impersonal institution. Almost all of the company staff live within walking distance of the theater. With the kind of day we have, one that ends after eleven in the evening for many of us, nothing else is sensible.

During the season, my daily routine doesn't change much. I wake at about eight (except on Mondays, the one day in the week we don't perform and when there are usually no classes or rehearsals) and can't say that I have a fine, substantial breakfast: what I have is coffee and juice. I read the newspaper, dance and theater reviews first, then tennis coverage, then the news. Since I live six blocks from the theater, I can leave my apartment at about ten-thirty to get to the eleven o'clock company class. Sometimes I leave earlier and warm up before class. Rehearsals begin at twelve, and if I am not scheduled for one, I might take Stanley Williams's men's class at SAB at twelve-thirty.

Rehearsals: I might be called for a new ballet, or to learn a new role, or to work with someone entering a ballet. Or I might have to supervise the rehearsals of one of my own works, or I might be making a ballet — or all of these at the same time. It is the job of our ballet mistress, Rosemary Dunleavy, to see that I am not scheduled to be in two places at the same time. She anticipates conflicts and will call me to discuss how one would best be solved.

As I've said, I have a reluctance about rehearsing for my own dancing. I know myself, and I know I have a tough time getting out there and performing. There are dancers who get so excited about performing that they put flowers in their hair, they paint their shoes, they fix their tights. Oh, they are so "into it." They can't wait for the evening performance to start. That's not me.

Since I have this reluctance, this strange kind of shyness (well, not always), I sometimes like to be not totally prepared just to leave the chance for something surprising to happen. I want to feel that I am not absolutely dead sure of what my partner will do, or what I will do. I know that at the least I'll dance accurately and partner conscientiously, but this slight area of being unprepared will allow me a place to invent and improvise, and also force me to concentrate harder. If I'm totally unsure, I'll rehearse. But it has seemed to me that the less I've manicured the role, the more interesting I am on stage. The mystery is whether the performance will be a great one, or a good one, or just routine. If it ends up being routine, I'll fall into a depression that will hang on for some time.

Of course, ultimately, only the performer is responsible for the outcome of any given performance, but there are elements he has no control over: the expectations and frame of mind of the audience, an eight-hour rehearsal

George Balanchine rehearsing Suzanne Farrell and P.M. in Chaconne (see also page 147) (© Martha Swope)

Jerome Robbins rehearsing Karin von Aroldingen and P.M. in The Goldberg Variations (© Martha Swope)

Jerome Robbins with Mikhail Baryshnikov, Jean-Pierre Frohlich, and P.M. in costume for Fancy Free (© Martha Swope)

Tango, with Natalia Makarova (© Jack Vartoogian)

With Mikhail Baryshnikov at Saratoga (© Steven Caras)

Stanley Williams, men's class at the School of American Ballet (right: © William Christensen)

George Balanchine teaching company class (© Steven Caras)

day behind him, an unfamiliar partner, inadequate orchestra playing, but probably, most importantly, an inflexible or indefinite conductor. Concentration must carry you through, and I know my task is to do it, and to think of nothing else but that. As a dancer, being on stage is the biggest responsibility you can have, and I try to perform full out no matter what the place or the size of the audience.

It is usually night when I learn where I'm supposed to be the next day, for the rehearsal schedule is actually not finalized until the end of the day, and then it is tape-recorded so the dancers can telephone in to find out where and when and for what they'll be needed. Checking that tape is what a dancer does before going to sleep (those who show up for rehearsals, that is!).

In our company you have to make a request for a personal rehearsal, asking for space and a pianist, for not all soloist and principal needs are anticipated. And you also have to ask someone to coach you in a role *you* are to dance but *he* knows. The rehearsal period extends usually to 6, though when the season gets going they can run up to performance time, and even later. If there is a break, and there might be one between 4 and 4:30, then I'll rush across the street to a hamburger joint for a cheeseburger and coffee. But however the day is filled, I am back in the theater at 7 (if I have ever left it) to put on makeup and warm up for the night's performance.

The warm-up barre is of your own devising, you do what you like and, more importantly, what you need. I prefer a long, slow warm-up, say some forty-five minutes to an hour, and the longer I take, the more thoroughly prepared I will feel and the longer I'll remain warm. This is important especially if I have to perform both in the first work on the program and the last one — with that slow and full preparation I'll still be warm by the end of the evening — and also I find that I'll tire less quickly if I do a long, slow barre. A warm-up includes the same things as a class: *plié*, lots of *tendu*, *ronds de jambe à terre*, *ronds de jambe en l'air*, *adagio*, *grand battement*, stretch, jumps — all of this depending on what you'll need in performance that night. Often this is done while the earlier ballets are going on, and you might do this in the side stage area, or in a studio above the stage.

Usually I'll stay throughout the entire performance even if I'm not performing, maybe to watch one of my own works or to study one of the others, or just to watch dancers. Sometimes I'll go out into the auditorium and stand at the back of the theater to see what a work looks like from out there. Dancers are always shocked when they see for the first time ballets they have danced in for years from the audience's view.

Performances end around 10:30, and we hang around a bit for some postmortem discussion — reviewing, criticizing each other, taking care of some business that wasn't finished during the day. When that is over, we socialize. (Who says dancers don't have time for socializing?) Most of my friends are dancers, or in a dance-related profession, and we meet at a nearby restaurant (we are habitués of some) and we'll gossip, argue, wonder if we'll ever be rich, but mostly eat and drink. Eating is a problem: during the season I try to stay away from desserts, but in fact the crowded day doesn't really allow me time to indulge a craving for a feast. I think dancers who do have a weight problem have it less for physiological reasons than for psychological ones. My list of do's and don't's for the season goes like this:

DO	DON'T
Get enough sleep	
Take class with Stanley	
Drink soda water with lime	Drink beer or wine in excess
Bum cigarettes from friends, if you must smoke, rather than buy a carton yourself	Smoke more than a pack a day, or a week, or during the whole season
Watch other companies, especially if you want to be grateful to be in the one you are in	Watch too many other companies, especially if you want to avoid depression

Eat veggies and fish	Eat cheesecake
Read critics	Take critics seriously
Gossip	Listen to gossip
Wash dance and practice clothes often	
	Rifle through the ballet mistress's desk
	Let ballerinas intimidate you
Read	Write a book

A dancer has to keep certain special considerations in mind when he is performing a large and varied repertory. In my own mind I have grouped ballets in various bizarre ways which have to do with such things as whether I have to use hair spray, how long a warm-up is required, or whether light or heavy makeup is needed. For instance, the morning of the day I perform *Tzigane* I can get away with not shaving since a stubble gives me a tougher look. In *Midsummer* I have to worry less about my hair being in place because I wear a cap.

The week before I'm to perform certain ballets is almost literally destroyed for me because of nervous anticipation of the work's difficulties. I smoke less, I sleep less, I eat less. They include *Mozartiana*, *Bournonville Divertissements*, *La Source*, *Tchaikovsky Pas de Deux*, *Raymonda Variations*, *Chaconne*. I could consider it some compensation that there are "holiday" ballets like *Union Jack* and *Vienna Waltzes* where warm-up consists of a warm cup of coffee and a "stale" danish.

Ballet shoes are a particular nuisance. I really focus hard on what I am to perform that night only two hours before the performance, when I walk into my dressing room from rehearsal and find my costume hanging there. I use approximately ten pairs of shoes a year (that's not many), five per season, and these are dyed and redyed to match the costume, a process dancers do themselves just before performance. I'm happy to be relieved of "dying responsibility" in the ballets *Duo Concertant*, *Violin Concerto*, and *Agon* because I wear socks over the shoes! Then there are the "gray shoe ballets" — *Tchaikovsky Pas de Deux*, *A Midsummer Night's Dream*, *Raymonda Variations*, *Swan Lake* — where the same pair will do, providing they still are without holes! Troublesome are the "bone-colored shoe ballets": *Diamonds*, *Chaconne*, *Bournonville Divertissements*, for they present a problem: you can dye bone to gray, but you can't go the other way, and so I have to reserve a special pair for these. Another relief group are those ballets where I wear boots: *Dances at a Gathering*, *Tzigane*, *Stars and Stripes*. Boots give me an immediate though not necessarily accurate feeling that these ballets are easier to perform.

To go on with my odd list, *Symphony in C* and *Scotch Symphony* are the only ballets where I wear black shoes, and *La Source* makes a maddening problem for me, for the tights are flesh-colored and the dye match is difficult to achieve.

During the season and out of season, it is my own responsibility to maintain my standard and my ability — dancers ruin themselves more often than are ruined by others — and I maintain myself by doing the most correct, most thought-out barres possible. A fantastic barre will keep me in working shape, and that, combined with the rehearsal and performance, should be sufficient to make up for a class missed because of lack of time.

The layoff time between seasons I use to correct and refine my technique, and to recondition myself. It's during that period I build for performances. Recently, I had the unusual experience of really being forced to rest, when my lower back completely gave way. After practically "living with" my chiropractor, I was cured by a combination of sleep, massage, rest, sleep, and, after a time, gentle swimming. When, after some four weeks of this regimen, I returned to class, I found my body had healed almost completely and that I had been brought back to working shape, paradoxically, by doing nothing. But the rule is more typically not to skip class for any length of time, and if you do not take class for more than three days, you'll need a week or more of daily classes before you are back in working shape.

Dancing demands a tremendous physical investment and a tremendous mental one, and you have to develop a self-knowing and self-judging sense very quickly. You have to be able to listen to yourself, criticize yourself, love yourself and comfort yourself, and you have to do this realistically and intelligently. You have to sieve out what isn't important and keep what is.

A feature of a good dancer is the ability to make fast choices, and this involves having another kind of dance intelligence, of an intellectual and conceptual sort. For example, a performer has to be alert in performance to be able to invent choreography in case another dancer stumbles or forgets. Also, learning a role involves an intellectual perception of the role's function within the work, and a grasp of the work's particular intention.

This intelligence is just what the general audience does not seem to credit dancers with. Dancing is as rigorous an intellectual discipline as it is a physical one. Yes, there are dumb dancers, but they are not good dancers.

A professional dancer's existence is filled with temptations (celebrity, money, travel), but the biggest one for a dancer is to let your ego take over. As important and as necessary as a healthy ego is, if you begin to treat your ego as the most important thing in the world, you place yourself at an impasse as a dancer. If your ego demands that everyone else and everything else be secondary to its needs, that everything must be at your service, you will be ruined as a dancer.

In specific terms, such egotists demand a company where they will be treated as an important personage, where someone will and must create for them, where their eccentricities will be welcomed and appreciated as a sign of divine mission, where unreliability will be indulged, where their delicacy, which doesn't allow a normal rehearsal schedule, will be catered to — or where they can rehearse and rehearse but not make a commitment to get out on stage and perform.

People have some odd conceptions and prejudices about dancing and the dance life. One is that the dancer is making some terrible sacrifice, a sacrifice that makes him or her, in the process, purer than everyone else. The choices a dancer makes, which include leaving things behind, do not necessarily involve sacrifice. You cannot talk about "sacrifice" when the rewards are simply so enormous. When you discover what it is that you value most, you don't lose. What you leave behind is probably best left behind. There is no sacrifice in personal relations. There are happy marriages, and there are unhappy ones, of all varieties, among dancers, and the fact of relationships surviving is in large part based on both partners being happy in what they do.

Are dancers inadequate in other life situations because of their self-imposed, sheltered life? Now, I feel very secure about who I am and what I do, and proud of being in this profession. This prideful assurance doesn't leave me when I meet people who are not in dance, or when the circumstance does not deal with the dance world. Because I feel adequate in that part of existence that I have chosen to concentrate on, I feel secure wherever I go.

I've heard people say dancers are vain and self-centered. A dancer's vanity comes from the fact that his body is his instrument, and it must be in the best shape to perform well. One has to be fearless with it, and take pride in it so that one presents the self completely. There isn't a separation between the body and mind when on stage. A dancer takes that intensity of physical presence with him at all times, in his carriage and in his manner. A dancer has to plead guilty of pride and self-concern. But it is wrong to name that vanity, for it comes from severe self-scrutiny that is uncompromising and never really assured. That dancers are concerned with who they are and how they appear is not remarkable, it seems to me.

Dancers are not obsessed by themselves — it is dancing they care about. And the best dancers are not obsessed by dancing, they are possessed by it.

CHAPTER SIX

Making Ballets

*T*oo *frequently,* dancers are asked what they will do when they can no longer perform. At times I've felt that there has been the condescending implication that what we are doing isn't a sufficiently adult occupation, that it is something you do when you are very young and it doesn't answer seriously the demands of real ambition. Most dancers, probably like most athletes, think the question will answer itself when the time comes, and indeed the immediate concerns are so overwhelming and so time consuming that planning for the future seems an absurd luxury.

When a dancer is injured so severely that there is a possibility that he will not be able to dance again, the shock is devastating — some of those for whom it has meant the end of a career never again look at a dance performance; they slide away from any contact with their dancer friends; they find a place where they were never known as dancers. What they have to do is remake their lives completely. But while this is a dramatic instance, it must happen to people in all kinds of careers, when hopes are dashed.

Even if there is no sudden end to a career, there are adjustments to be made all along the way, and the major one comes when you know just what your level is going to be. Just how far can you develop? Will you be an outstanding technician and nothing else? Will you develop the strength needed for certain technical challenges? Can you find your own identity as an artist? There comes the time when you know you'll never have solo parts, that what you are and always will be is a member of the corps, that if you want solo roles you are going to have to find a small company. However, I know many dancers who just give up too early, who don't fight hard and long enough, who trust to the opinion of others, who don't pass the test of being strong willed.

But even if you do not attain the goal you aimed for as a dancer, the compensation is that you are dancing and doing exactly what you want to do, and to hell with applause and fame.

At the end of a dancing career, the options for those who want to remain in the field are few. There are teaching and coaching, of course; maybe managing a company, or working as a ballet master. With guts you can start your own company, and you can choreograph. But choreography isn't something you just take up — except in my case.

I've been lucky in having the luxury to explore what might be possible for myself. I long ago accepted that all of my life was going to be devoted to dance, that my existence involves dancing in whatever way I can best contribute. My privilege is that within the structure of the New York City Ballet I can try my skill at making dances — that I can choreograph. With each new work I make, I challenge myself and test my capabilities. One work leads to the next, and in my mind there are discussions between the pieces I make: here is a partnering challenge, here is a design for a small troupe, here for a large mass. The music determines the style of the particular work, and what I don't think about is My Style, just as I never worried about My Style as a dancer.

My young ambition was to be a star, to make a big name for myself, and I would easily achieve this by being the most perfect, the most precise, the surest dancer in the world. I would be the best at what I did, and frankly I thought little about any competition. I had no choreographic ambitions, and it wasn't part of my early training to think that the top job was being a choreographer. I often think that the cult of the "choreographer" is almost an American view.

Every good dancer is, in part, a choreographer, for the ability to manipulate the given choreography, to reimbue it with life and originality, to shape the work to the dancer's special qualities is an indication of the dancer's intelligence. When that concern is extended beyond the dancer's self-concern to creating movement for others, the first move to being a choreographer has occurred.

Dancers always imagine combinations of steps in their mind. That is the stuff of class, and since you spend every day shaping movements to the sound of music, when you hear music you automatically "see" steps. You make up ballets on the bus, or just before falling asleep, and you imagine wonderful things that you can do, that others you care about, or interest you, can do.

176

My first try in making design for movement was in Copenhagen for a fashion show. I don't remember much of what I did, but I do know that I meant to be outrageous. It had some effect, for the experience didn't dissuade me from thinking about staging and choreography.

When I came to the United States, I was too uninformed to understand fully the privilege of working with the most respected of living choreographers, George Balanchine and Jerome Robbins, but I was told soon enough how remarkable my situation was. They were more famous and more revered than any dancer in their company, or for that matter in any American company. They were it! And not being unambitious myself, I wondered if I could do what they did, whether maybe I had a tiny bit of genius. (For all I knew, all famous choreographers were geniuses. I discovered differently later.) Another kind of schooling began, for not only was I learning roles in the works of these masters, I was learning their solutions to the problems of dance.

In late 1976, the New York City Ballet orchestra went on strike, and we dancers could not perform at our home theater. For a small program at Brooklyn College I gathered a small company to dance pieces from the NYCB repertory. Suzanne Farrell and I appeared in roles we were noted for, but the rest of the program offered a chance for the younger dancers to do roles they hadn't performed with the company, and I asked Richard Tanner and Robert Weiss, dancers with choreographic ambitions, to make new pieces. Weiss picked a Fauré work. Tanner selected Schubert songs, and he also wanted to work on some short orchestral pieces by Charles Ives. Dick was working on the Schubert but was having trouble completing it in time, and maybe as a friendly challenge, he suggested that I take over some of the Ives pieces. The music seemed ugly and fascinating and quirky and funny, so I agreed, and began to work.

Though the NYCB wasn't performing, there was a full rehearsal schedule, and Jerome Robbins was working on a big piece, *Arts of the Gentleman* — this was at the experimental, workshop stage. So the small troupe I had arranged would rehearse in our spare time, mostly in the evening. Alone, I worked out some steps for about two hours for the Ives work, and then Daniel Duell, whom we asked to dance the work, arrived and I showed him what I had just made.

When Dick saw how far along I had come, and how quickly I had moved to the assignment, he just threw up his hands in mock despair and said I should do the whole thing. I was left with the feeling that I had been backed into making a ballet, even though I probably hadn't. Now that I had these dances on my hands, I thought I needed a title, and I looked in the most appropriate place for one, on the record jacket. The title I liked best was "Calcium Light Night," and I rushed to correct an omission — I hadn't choreographed that particular piece.

The premiere in Brooklyn was a hit with the audience. Maybe from my sense that this was all an experiment, I used the open stage, leaving the back pipes and brick exposed, and Danny Duell wandered about as if what he was doing was being improvised. Perhaps this was all a little affected, but it saved the cost of making a set and worrying over a costume. It looked Very Modern.

But the piece didn't seem complete to me, and I felt it was a work that hadn't found its full form. One thought I had was that I wanted to add new pieces to the work for Heather Watts, a dancer from whom I had learned about American style, and the woman I was romantically involved with. Having worked through a series of solos, I wanted to try a duet. For a next engagement of the small group, in Seattle, I selected more Ives pieces, including "Halloween," which Balanchine had used in his 1954 Ives ballet *Ivesiana* but which was dropped in revivals of that work. I made the additional solos for Heather and two duets for Danny and Heather.

The company manager, Edward Bigelow, heard about this performance and told Mr. Balanchine that I had had a success with a ballet. Just before the spring season, with the musician's strike settled, Balanchine came to me and said, "I hear you did something, dear. Can I see?" I told him it wasn't much, that I was just doodling around. He shook his head and said no, he must see, and we arranged to meet the next day in a practice room of the School of American Ballet at Juilliard.

Still, I felt the work was lacking something, and a half-hour before Mr. Balanchine arrived I added yet another new piece for Heather ("At Sea"), for I was looking for an additional mood, something less sharp and acid than the other sections.

When Balanchine came in, we behaved as if we'd just been trying out a few things, which indeed we had, but Heather and Danny and I were in a fit of mild terror. He sat down, without expression, without fuss, and I stood at his side a few feet away. I turned on the tape and Danny and Heather went through the work without stopping, and without a sign from Balanchine.

At the end, he stood up and came over to me.

"You know, wonderful."

"Really?" In spite of Brooklyn and Seattle, I had no sense that I had made anything of any substance.

"Excellent. When did you do?"

"A few months ago."

He told me what he liked: it was musical, odd, interesting; and he asked if I had any costumes. Well, I told him, I knew exactly what I wanted it to look like.

"Good, we'll do opening night. Okay? So long, dear."

Some fourteen days later, *Calcium* was premiered in New York, and the reviewers announced that I was a choreographer.

It might partly be because the actual making of this work was in the nature of an experiment that I wanted to keep the feel of a laboratory about it, and Steven Rubin's set was a bare stage, with a hovering square of neon, the calcium light night. The costumes cling like metal casing, severe. All this accents the sharp angularities of the music. The music is cracked, and so is the choreography and the world this dance describes. It is some place full of lunacy, an acrobatic lunacy.

It begins with a series of solos for the boy, after which the girl enters and the boy leaves. The music for the fourth piece is repeated, and she dances, on point, a version of the boy's choreography. Two more solos for the girl, and then the two duets, the final one to "Halloween."

Two years later, this piece was filmed for television, with Heather and Ib Andersen in the boy's role. That is a real test of a work's vitality, when a new dancer takes over a role — then you see if the separation can be made: the dance from the dancer. How and in what ways does the role exist? Is something crucial lost when the first dancer leaves, or is the role a vessel that can be filled in a number of ways? There are dances that simply collapse once a particular dancer is gone, once that dancer doesn't supply what is missing from the choreography.

Among the hallmarks of a well-made piece is that its overall design is so secure that one can tamper with individual steps without harming the total effect. This tolerance for some variety in stress and interpretation gives breadth to a ballet. I have seen some roles go absolutely dead for years, and then a dancer comes along and finds it again, makes the work live again. Within the repertory of the NYCB you could write long biographies of certain roles, of how they sparkled when this one danced the part, went drab for years when So-and-So marked his way through it, and then arrived young So-and-So and found treasures. Mr. Balanchine revives his older ballets when he has dancers who can do justice to them: he revived *Prodigal Son* for Edward Villella; *Ballet Imperial* (now called *Tchaikovsky Concerto No. 2*) for Patricia McBride, and recently Merrill Ashley has been especially remarkable in it.

The success of *Calcium* didn't assure me that I was a full-fledged choreographer. By no means. It is easy to make a first ballet, I think, and it was easy for me, for the thoughts and ideas behind *Calcium* had been accumulating ever since I had come to the United States. In many ways, *Calcium* is a statement of my perception of American manners and American character — it is in a modern American idiom — or maybe it's just "very Heather."

Whether I am a choreographer will be proved when I have produced

Calcium Light Night: (left, top and bottom) choreographing and rehearsing with Heather Watts and Daniel Duell; (right top) in performance; (right bottom) Heather Watts (left, and right top, © Martha Swope; right bottom, © Steven Caras)

Rossini Pas de Deux, with Heather Watts and Sean Lavery (© Martha Swope)

Tricolore, with Colleen Neary and Adam Lüders (© Martha Swope)

Choreographing Sonate di Scarlatti, with Heather Watts and Bart Cook (© Steven Caras)

Sonate di Scarlatti, with Heather Watts and Bart Cook (© Martha Swope)

Choreographing Lille Suite, with Heather Watts and Ib Andersen (© Carolyn George)

Lille Suite, with Heather Watts and Ib Andersen
(© Martha Swope)

Eight Easy Pieces, with Stacy Caddell, Susan Gluck, Roma Sosenko (top: © Steven Caras; bottom: © Martha Swope)

a body of work, and when my work exhibits depth and a distinctive character. I felt that strongly then, and I knew that I'd make up my mind after four works, or six, or twenty, maybe, or . . .

I was euphorically happy at this first success and all the fuss, and all the surprised "Well, I didn't think you could do anything" comments, but I didn't get any wild notions that I was the new great genius or anything. No inflated self-importance (but there was the fantasy), I confess, that maybe someday I would make a great ballet that would live through the ages! Those thoughts were daydreams, and I pasted the reviews in my little scrapbook, and a neat bunch was sent off to my mother, and with that out of the way I settled down to earth.

Naturally, I had to find a way to be discontented about something, and I griped that after all these long hard years trying to make some impact as a dancer, here I was unappreciated, ignored, and overlooked. Then suddenly I make a few little steps, and my name is listed among the ranks of choreographers, and now everyone is making a fuss and wants to interview me. How ironic! How depressing!

This need for approval — and then when it comes the need to deny its validity or real justice — works like a spur to keep me moving, to leave me always dissatisfied and anxious to move on. Before the Ives premiere I had settled on trying to make a *pas de deux* to Rossini piano pieces, music as far away from the dissonances and oddities of Ives as I could get. It would be a romantic piece; I wanted to show Heather in a different mood and aspect.

She suggested Sean Lavery as a partner, and he agreed to join us and see what I could come up with. (Not all dancers want to waste time being experimented on by untried choreographers. In dance, there is no real "free" or extra time. Time is precious and you have to pick carefully what you do with it.)

In four days I put together an extended *pas de deux*, to selections from Rossini's "Sins of My Old Age." On that fourth day, Jerome Robbins peeked into the studio, and we all stared at each other.

"What are you doing?"

"Oh, I'm just playing around, making something just for the fun of it."

"Can I watch?"

"Sure." After five minutes he left, just waved and out he went.

That was in February, and some weeks later, Mr. Balanchine told me that Jerry was planning a Sketchbook for the upcoming spring season, with excerpts from his works in progress, a section from a piece to Verdi ballet music, and studies from his long contemplated *Arts of the Gentleman.*

"Jerry tells me you choreographed a nice, pretty duet. Have you finished?"

"Yes."

Without asking to see it, he said, "Then we'll put it in."

I knew the *pas de deux* was a bit long, but I didn't know how to fix it by cutting. The company pianist, Gordon Boelzner, and the company conductor, Robert Irving, assured me there wasn't anything holy about this music, and it was no big deal to cut it, but I didn't know what it was that should be dropped. Finally, I asked Balanchine to come and take a look and give me his suggestions.

Now, I repeat his compliments not from bragging but because his words are among the most wonderful ever said to me. They come as a gift, and as a proof of his love for dance. Like the generous encourager, like the kind parent, he always seems to like what I do — rather, almost always: there are times when he vanishes too, when he seems to want to unsettle me, but those tales are for another time.

This time he said, "It's wonderful. You know, it's not sentimental, that's what's good about it. But the ending, well, there is something not right there. We'll have to fix the ending a little bit, something is not right. I understand what you want to do, but maybe you should work a little bit on the ending."

"What should I do?"

Ten minutes later, he had finished rechoreographing a section just before the ending and had remade it so that it had some impact. It set up the ending better, thereby improving the ending itself. He asked Heather and Sean to do my version, and then follow it with his. After that, he asked me which I preferred.

"Yours."

"Why?"

"Well, it doesn't make any more sense, but it has more surprises, like it's less logical and because of that more surprising, as if I didn't know what would happen next."

"Then it is yours, for free." And he patted my arm, and off he went, with a cute smug expression.

This is a complex relationship, that of master and student, and I cannot pretend it is all simple and without fear, distrust and suspicion as well as affection, reverence, gratitude. My choreographic tutelage has not been an easy one — choreographers usually start at a younger age than I did. Through all my griping I knew that I was a noted dancer, that I had finally established myself in one place, just, and here I was embarking on being something else, courting failure, insisting once again that nothing be easy.

It didn't help that the example before me was the greatest choreographer probably of all time, that I was dancing in his masterpieces, and that no matter what disclaimers are made, there is always competition — one is always measuring one's own achievement against someone else's. At the suggestion of criticism I fight and resist, and then am grateful for even the smallest praise, then fierce in my pride and brave through an assurance that isn't always there. What a fury of emotions — and it strikes me that in a calmer, clearer world nothing would happen to me, that I wouldn't be compelled to move myself to do things. Yet I must insist that the kind of career I have had as a dancer or choreographer would not have been possible without Balanchine's influence.

I am not psychoanalytical per se, but I know that growing up without a father has made me overly sensitive to father figures, and frantic for their approval, as if I weren't sure what such a relationship consisted of. I feel

191

as if I've inherited a destiny as a dancer, and only later did I find out that I could make myself up, become whomever I wanted to be.

Like all members of the company, I studied this man who molded my career first by ignoring me and punishing me, then by paying attention, and by encouraging the budding choreographer. I learned to read all his words and looks. And I think I know him well — if anyone will ever know George Balanchine. I know when he is giving people a runaround, a song and dance. I know when he is talking too much in order to hide his real thoughts, when what he really means is being revealed by what he isn't saying. I have seen him when he is ruggedly, brutally honest — and then when by being courteously polite he is being enigmatic. When he doesn't approve, he prefers to remain silent, and if he is forced to make a comment, it will be abrupt and cryptic.

In the spring of 1979, Balanchine was recovering from an illness, and I worked in collaboration with him on two projects: a section of an unsuccessful work, *Tricolore* — the other sections were made by Jean-Pierre Bonnefous and Jerome Robbins — and a ballet for the New York City Opera's production of *Dido and Aeneas*, both of these journeyman works meant for an occasion and not for the ages — or at least that's what happened. My choreographic experiences were mounting up and this gave me the courage to tell Mr. Balanchine that my interest in choreographing was serious, and gave me also the courage to admit this to myself. Even though I was dancing every night, I wanted to have a choreographic project of my own. I wanted to tackle something major.

Was there any particular composer, I asked him, whose work would be good for me to work on at this point? Should I try a Tchaikovsky piece?

"You know something, dear. Scarlatti, interesting composer. I always wanted to do myself. I never had time."

This suggestion I took as an injunction, a command, and for two hours in the morning and two hours at night for six months I listened to recordings of Scarlatti sonatas for harpsichord. Finally, I made a selection and arranged them so that there would be a structure suitable for a full ballet.

It would be a work for ten dancers, with Heather and Bart Cook in the lead roles. At this point I was worried about my always using Heather. I didn't want it to appear as favoritism, for we were a "team" offstage, and the seeming nepotism was unfair to my respect for her talent, but she was in fact the dancer I preferred. I asked Mr. Balanchine what he thought and he assured me that since she was the one I knew best, both as a person and a dancer, it was only natural to choose her for parts.

With this work, I deliberately set out to challenge my range as a choreographer. This would be an essay in combinations: two duets for two boys, then two duets for two girls. After the entrance and presentation, there were solos, girls in pairs, boys in pairs, then two central *pas de deux.*

Though this was all a formal working through, what I was really working out was my facility in detail work, an effort to extend my flexibility and the dancers' too in the demonstration of classical vocabulary.

The pairing of duets made me find two solutions to the same problem, and I was confining myself to all sorts of problems. (For instance, there were *two* dances for two boys, and I was therefore forced to make each boy duet different from the other — so there were two solutions to the same choreographic problem.) Here too I meant to show my ability to use space on stage, through geometrical designs. The boys cut diagonals across the stage, then make circles, a straight line from up to down stage, then a semicircle. The audience is meant to see and to feel too these design patterns and exercises.

I was showing these ten dancers in as many combinations as made sense, giving everyone the chance to show his or her technical range. And when these possibilities end, so does the ballet. Therefore, the ballet is an exercise and is meant to have the logic of an exercise.

The ballet was premiered in Saratoga, during the company's annual summer season, and this allowed me to work on it before it was exposed to the New York audience. After the ballet had been made, I thought it might look good in a set, but I wanted nothing too specific. From the scenery room, I selected a stripped-down version of a set first made for

Balanchine's *Divertimento No. 15*, a garden trellis that once had also served in Jerome Robbins's ballet to Stravinsky's *Dumbarton Oaks* and has probably spent time in some other works too. The costumes for the girls were pretty dresses. Lincoln Kirstein liked my idea to title the work *Giardino di Scarlatti*, but title, costumes and set didn't please Mr. Balanchine. All these elements were discarded before the New York premiere, and the new name was *Sonate di Scarlatti*. *Giardino*, he said, sounded like an Italian restaurant.

Balanchine pointed out to me that I hadn't begun the ballet with a garden party in mind, and that if I had, the whole work would have been different. Maybe, he said, you would have choreographed it differently and shown us a garden. As it was, I was misrepresenting the piece, smothering it in an alien notion. He vetoed another idea I had: I had wanted the sonatas, which were written for harpsicord, re-arranged for an orchestra, but he said that a piano would be sufficient.

Another occasion when he vetoed me again was over the casting of the next piece I choreographed, a little work, made at Balanchine's suggestion for a benefit gala for the Library of the Performing Arts at Lincoln Center, to Stravinsky's *Eight Easy Pieces* for two pianos. At its premiere it was played by the duo pianists Arthur Gold and Robert Fizdale. Balanchine was pleased with the result, and he added it to the NYCB repertory. My first intention was to use three of the ballerinas in the company, but Balanchine said no: they had to be young, little girls, the babies. (For the record, they were Stacy Caddell, Roma Sosenko and Susan Gluck.) I can only guess at what he intended: perhaps to keep the work young and sweet, to strengthen my ties to the company's young members, or perhaps just not to waste his ballerinas?

During the last week of August of 1980, the company was scheduled to appear at Tivoli in Copenhagen, and as a tribute to Denmark, George Balanchine asked me in the spring before to make a work to Carl Nielsen's *Lille Suite*, Opus 1, a work he had vague recollections of and whose score I had scouted out for him on one visit home. I thought at first the music sounded a little meandering and sweet, and I hoped that during the summer

194

he'd forget about it. But in the middle of July, during the height of our Saratoga season, he asked me how much of it I had completed. I told him that I hadn't started, but that I had all my ideas together in my head so it would be no problem at all to set it very quickly — and then I went off to look around for my ideas. Balanchine suggested that it be like the Tivoli fountains, and I have a big corps of girls who would be dancing waters (well, it was a beginning!).

The lead couple was to be Suzanne Farrell and the newest Dane to join the NYCB, Ib Andersen, but after I made the first minute on Suzanne she disappeared (maybe she had a fear of water) and Heather offered to replace her. The Tivoli world premiere was a big success, for it was a work by a native son, starring another native boy made good, and it was dedicated to the Director of Tivoli, Niels-Jørgen Kaiser. It was seen in New York on the the opening night of the company's Fall 1980 season.

There is no story behind *Lille Suite*, but the music suggested to me some ideas about the progress of love, and the ballet is a kind of little love story. In the first movement the boy and girl are very passionate, full of the passion you feel when you first fall in love. In the second movement, they are happy, expressing the joys of love. But in the third movement trouble comes, and they tear at each other. The ballet ends with the lovers parting, but they are parting together; the decision is a mutual one.

The next piece Balanchine had in mind for me was Stravinsky's *Suite from Histoire du Soldat*, a work which seems to have defeated every choreographer, and a work which Mr. Balanchine has himself never set. (I wonder why.)

I'll describe the making of this piece to give an idea what the choreographic process consists of.

The company's main rehearsal room is on the top floor of the backstage area of the New York State Theater, and it is a windowless, large room whose size bears no relation to the size of the stage. The front wall is mirrored, and to its left, cater-cornered, is the piano. The room is outlined at waist height by a barre, and there are a few folding chairs of proven discomfort scattered about. The light is bleached fluorescent, and though Mr. Balanchine is a confirmed and proselytizing nonsmoker, there is a tin ashtray stand. Above, ceiling leaks have loosed the acoustic tiles.

In essentials, the form and elements of this room are exactly those of all the dance areas of a dancer's life: the classrooms, the practice rooms, the rehearsal rooms. They are all the same, and it is among these spaces that dancers shuttle. Its ultimate form is the stage itself, the mirror yielding to a proscenium.

Everything happens in this space: you learn to dance, you learn roles, you perform. And when you aren't in the center of the room, you sit on the sides, drinking a soda, eating cookies (or health bars), smoking, doing the crossword puzzle, reading, gossiping, catching up on sleep, sewing your shoes, stretching to a split.

A dancer's complexion often reflects that sunless, sweaty, confined environment, but the concentration and seeming sacrifice are to a point, and that point is joy. Granted I'm a biased commentator, but I can't think of a better, happier existence than that of a dancer. The world is competitive, nervous, full of animosity and disappointments, but overall this is a world full of the thrill of movement, of shaping movement, of doing something so absorbing, so totally involving that it uses every part of you. As dancers, we must be alive at every moment, and what we do is by its nature deliriously invigorating.

Though I count myself a Stravinsky fan, his *Histoire* suite isn't a piece I would have selected at that point for myself. But it was a considered choice, and though it set me against an incomparable composer/choreographer standard (in ballet Stravinsky's name is linked with Balanchine), I agreed.

As it is, I am learning the craft in a glass bowl and in reviews am pitted against masters. I don't have the luxury of working in secret and perfecting something before I expose it, or working in a city that isn't the dance capital of the world. I can't make a dismissible work, for each is treated as my latest and most important statement, and every effort is judged as if this were the work that says whether or not I have talent. On the other hand, there isn't a moment when I'm not aware of the privilege I have, and I am not long distracted from the work at hand. So why not try a big Stravinsky piece? I'm in an extraordinarily difficult place already, and cowardice won't make it easier. As I always say, go for it!

The process begins with listening to the music until the work lives within me, until I have made the work a part of me. The suite is arranged from Stravinsky's theater piece *Histoire du Soldat*, the story of the devil and a soldier in which the devil finally triumphs and carries off the soldier's soul. Happily for a choreographer, the music includes marches, tangos, waltzes, ragtime, and a chorale that I used as a processional.

Stravinsky made this piece for a small orchestra, and the instrumental voices are brilliantly opposed, and these contrasts make another character for dance to work on. But it is Stravinsky's rhythmical variety that makes his music so wonderfully suggestive for a choreographer, and in this piece the writing becomes so spare in places that it feels as if the only thing you are working with *is* rhythm. Maybe it is in this play of rhythm that you find the central pulse of the work that will carry the choreographic design. I think a choreographer has to trust his instinct for finding this pulse of the work.

Having a secure idea of the musical shape of the piece by taking all these elements into consideration will establish the stylistic identity of the piece. This means that once you have absorbed the musical style you will know immediately, perhaps even intuitively, which steps will be a match for this music and which ones won't. Certain choreographic patterns will seem appropriate: perhaps severe lines for classical music, or elaborate patterns for baroque, or angular shapes and asymmetrical forces for modern music. The music suggests the number of dancers you will use, and the kind of dancers you need, those who project a romantic image or those whose dance attack is sharp, for instance.

197

For each section of the suite, I decided, well, this will be for all boys; and this a *pas de deux*; and this a girl's solo with a small corps of girls; this for a girl and three boys. At the same time, the music dictated a mood or style, and a specific shape for the section: teasing and flirtatious with skips; sharp footwork suggesting a hard brilliance; or buffoonish. Then I had to think through the arrangement of the pieces — how the sections are juxtaposed so that there is dance variety, in the number of dancers in each section and in the dance steps used, but not so much diversity as to tear apart some unifying undercurrent that will hold the parts together. This undercurrent should emerge from the work's central impulse. The music itself will provide the coherency, and in a sense you have to have blind faith that it is there and that you have been responsive to it.

I try to come to rehearsal with a scheme already determined, so as not to waste my time and the dancers', or to try their patience with my confusion. There will be a general idea, in the best of circumstances, and then I'll have to modify it to the dancers' personalities, abilities, and suggestions. Sometimes I arrive with no idea at all, and I get to work, not waiting for any inspiration, just pushing myself through until inspiration or whatever it is that gives me ideas gets going.

I disregarded the dramatic text of *Histoire* (the suite uses all the music) and any of the character and action implications in the music, except for those that are embedded in the music, like the music parodies. To match the various moods, drawn as the instrumental lines are, clear and brilliant and quick, I decided to use a large cast, where the number of soloists is almost equal to the number of corps. At one point in the dance these two forces mirror each other.

Having cast the ballet with the assistance of the ballet mistress, Rosemary Dunleavy (who'll tell me who is available and who might not be), I began rehearsals not with the entire cast but by working each section individually. I had to trust that the whole piece would hang together eventually, though I knew there would be adjustments when it was ready to be run through. The whole choreographic process, creating and all rehearsals, was limited to forty-five hours.

Since I am a dancer, I dance out the roles I choreograph, trying pretty much everything on myself to see if it can be done, or figuring out how it can be done without breaking a leg. Since we have all been schooled in this dance vocabulary for years, we share a shorthand and a quickness to guess what the other means, and I'll sketch a movement with my body, saying, "Now, do dah de dah de dah de dum." There will be little use of the French terms to describe steps (since my vocabulary is limited to *plié* and *entrechat-six*), though at a later stage I'll be joined by an assistant who will write the steps down in a notebook, not in any of the dance notations, but in the long form describing as thoroughly as she can what is happening. These notes will serve not only as a memory aid to me, but will enable this assistant to cover rehearsals and cast changes when I'm not available. The ballet mistress too will join the rehearsals and learn the ballet to help in coaching. She will especially make herself alert to the corps needs.

Being a dancer with the same company you are making a ballet on can be a problem, especially when you might be pushing around the dancer who some few hours ago you were dancing with. The role of choreographer demands authority, and the yielding of authority by dancers to co-equals doesn't come that easily. I've never choreographed a role for myself and don't intend to. As a dancer, I'm used to being the instrument of a choreographer, and I find it impossible to perform both functions; besides, I like to see what I've made.

Dance companies are stratified, not only in management but in categories of dancers, and companies breed camps. The NYCB is made up of an unusually vocal, noisy, bright, and gossipy group. They are also the most professional. Sometimes I think I have overstressed a temperamental severity to get the kind of discipline and attention that I think I must have. Rehearsals can get tense, and within the short time allotted to make a new work, conflicts are unavoidable.

Dancers will give me corrections and tell me that what I've asked for is impossible, unsuitable, unmusical. They will complain that my steps will make them bump into each other or get tangled in each others' limbs. One dancer will show me how he has rechoreographed what I gave him the day before. "See, isn't this much better?" Or someone will come over to point out that I'm not counting the music correctly. "You see? This is how it goes." Or I'll catch in the mirror two dancers mocking a passage I've just given them, or looking at me as if I've obviously just gone completely out of my mind, or yawning with the boredom of it all. Since I'm still a dancer myself this doesn't bother me at all — if anything, I'm sympathetic.

Quick anger and anxiety, and quick back to work, getting all the nonsense out of the way. Another quality that has been bred into dancers is an enormous sense of humor. Dancers are mimics and cut-ups, jokesters, self-parodists. They are the quickest to laugh of anyone I know. A sense of humor is what keeps all this in place, and when all gets too tense, I become Mr. Superpatient, light up a cigarette, keep calm.

The NYCB dancers have grown up together, and many share apartments. That doesn't mean they are one big happy family. They are like most families: squabbling, discontented, jealous, going through phases, changing. But all this is evidence of a firm bonding, a common purpose and ambition. The head of the household is Mr. Balanchine, and no matter what our separate functions, and our separate achievements, our relationship to the company as a whole and our relation to each other is in considerable measure determined by our relationship to him.

A company pianist will work with me through the making of the ballet, and he will memorize key moments of the choreography so that he will know where in the music he has to turn to when I ask to repeat passages of the choreography. I might ask to try again, for instance, a passage beginning with a lift. My references to places I want to cover again will be made in terms of dance steps, not musical phrases. The pianist has to be sensitive to the choreographer's needs in counting the music, advising on repeats and which passages might be safely cut, anticipating changes in tempo, and indicating what orchestral instruments are playing the music we are hearing just on the piano. During the making of a ballet I keep a tape of the orchestral version with me. Mr. Balanchine is celebrated for being a trained musician and therefore able to make his own piano reductions of the full orchestral scores for the rehearsal period, and for making them for choreographers who have worked with him.

When the ballet is complete, our conductors, Robert Irving and Hugo Fiorato, will watch a run-through, and we'll discuss the tempos. If there is a disagreement, the argument will be carried to Mr. Balanchine and we might consult recordings by preferred conductors.

All the movement has to be counted to the music. The dancers' counts are not the same ones found in the musical score, of course. Dancers are cuing their entrances and exits to what the other dancers are doing, for one thing, and they are "counting" steps not notes.

With Stravinsky, the very compactness of the musical score (the amount of intense invention in the shortest space) insists on choreographic variety. The changes in tempo and shifts in instrumental coloration often demand that I make more steps. The problem then becomes one of over-loading a ballet with movement, and there is the danger of losing an overall shapeliness by working in so much minute-by-minute detail.

A solution is not to invent movement for all you hear, but instead to just keep the dancers in one place during certain sections, or to ignore the music, or use it as a background. Not making any steps is precisely what I did as an introduction to the finale — everyone marches on.

One of the subjects of my ballet to *Histoire*, it became clear early on, was the dancers themselves (it probably is the subject of all ballets). My choices of which dancers for which sections already implied a statement of my thoughts about their dancing and their *dance* personalities. For Heather's sections, I was thinking about her wit, her camaraderie, her high spirits, and her acuteness in accenting and timing. Here, she dances with three boys, and words describing what these four dancers are all doing here would include flirting, loving, quarreling, teasing, competing — they are an elegant and maybe slightly irritating group, bratty and playful and funny.

Inevitably, what is being captured in *Histoire* is a moment in their careers, and how I perceive them and their present strengths and concerns as dancers. The audience probably senses the intimacy of a friend making a work for his friends; I think that feel of personal involvement does spill over, even as an unconscious presence. Maybe. Necessarily, then, in some strong way the work will be changing in a year's time — the steps will be the same, but the way they are performed will be different.

The first rehearsals are easy and friendly, and the opening seems far away, unimaginable. The beginning work is full of exploration and subject to total change, and what the entire piece will look like isn't certain at all to the dancers!

We all start to become concerned about two weeks before the opening, when the parts are assembled and the fine-tuning begins, with countless repetitions of the same material. The choreography suddenly strikes all of us as not so impossible as it was the other day, but almost facile — *or* it continues to seem impossible so that the work is a trap that is going to show dancers and choreographer as inept. This is all happening in the rehearsal room, and it is almost as if the work itself were anxious to get on stage and get it all over with already. I am waiting to be told by the ballet mistress when the stage itself will be available for rehearsal.

The premiere of *Histoire* is to take place in the latter part of the winter season, when all of the ballets scheduled for that season are being performed in repertoire, when the stage is available for rehearsal only for what is being performed that night. It may be barely a few days before the opening of any ballet that the work will first be tried on the stage itself.

Doubts come heavy: is the music a hopeless bog? Don't the dancers seem lackluster and uninvolved? Is there any genuine inventiveness here?

Has no one anything to tell me about what I've done? Will Mr. Balanchine come in with last-minute suggestions, finally undermining any sense of what I set out to do? Why are the dancers smirking so much?

We move to the stage, and what we find is that nothing fits — either the design is too small to fill the space, or the dancers' exits appear to be happening in the middle of the stage rather than at the sides. What had been a circular pattern in the studio flattens out to an ellipse on stage. The work is transformed because of this change of setting, and the dancers start to dance with a sense of an audience. All details are sharpened; their dancing personae emerge. They dance bigger, and they project their dancing.

The orchestral rehearsal is an amazement. We have not heard sounds like these before — it bears no relation to what our sympathetic, agreeable pianist has been doing, or to anything we've heard on tape. Either it is deadly slow, or impossibly fast, and when the dancers exit, they are exhausted either from trying to sustain their dancing over dragging tempos or from trying to rush in all the steps that used to fit when the music was played a bit more slowly. Eight bars in the piano score, to be played by the trumpet in the orchestrated version, becomes three bars in performance when Mr. Hornblower forgets to "enter on time."

While these shocks are hitting us, the lighting designer is flashing colors, and there are prayers all around that these costumes must be a joke or a big mistake, and we all start rummaging in our minds through the costumes we remember from other ballets in our repertory to replace these.

With Ronald Bates, the lighting designer, I've worked out a lighting plot for each section of the work, naming hot tones like pinks and purples and reds as the controls. Ben Benson has shown me costume sketches and we've run through swatches of material. The celebrated Italian designer Valentino has created a special costume for Heather, and has had it flown to us. Beautifully made as it is, its very elegance makes too much of a disruptive effect, and it is dropped.

At the final dress rehearsal, you can hear the sound of scissors snipping away fringes on the costumes, the gels are switched to temper the lighting, the corps is pushed slightly downstage to avoid collisions, and I'm humming to the conductor to show the tempo I need.

No one is certain what has been made, and we are waiting for the audience to tell us how pleased or uninterested they are.

A new ballet will live through a season no matter what the reviews, and reviews from the weeklies and monthlies drift in slowly. It will take some two weeks or more to be able to gather a critical consensus, and that is just as well, for by then I have seen the work in a number of performances and have a surer sense of what I think. I'm sometimes informed and puzzled by criticism, but I rely on my own opinion. Whatever the reviews, I'm ready to move on.

Some of the reviews complained, however, that it was coolly intellectual, witty, considered it a well-wrought exercise that perhaps lacked a heart. I'm waiting to look at it objectively in a year's time, but for now I am sure that I have done it exactly as I wished to have done it. I know it is an advance over what I've made before, and that I am shedding the hesitancies and mistakes of the first-time choreographer. The reviewers are the first to notice this, and they call glibness what I feel is assurance. Every once in a while (actually, I think, quite often) a critic will name a piece of garbage a masterpiece. With luck, that same critic will find my pieces hopeless.

While I was working on *Histoire*, plans had already been under way for a Tchaikovsky festival that Balanchine had named as the major event of the Spring 1981 season, and he had begun handing out assignments. Mine was the First Symphony, but he mentioned another work that he would like me to make, a piece for the annual workshop performance of the School of American Ballet, and he said that if I had nothing better to do during the layoff between the winter and spring seasons, I could fit this in.

This was a new version of a ballet that Mr. Balanchine had appeared in as a very young man, *The Magic Flute*, with a score by Riccardo Drigo.

Rehearsing Suite from Histoire du Soldat, with Darci Kistler (© Martha Swope)

Suite from Histoire du Soldat, (top left) with Bart Cook, Heather Watts, and Daniel Duell;
(bottom) with Kyra Nichols, Darci Kistler, Helene Alexopoulos, Maria Calegari, Heather Watts; (top right) with Darci Kistler and Ib
Andersen (top left and bottom: © Steven Caras; top right: © Martha Swope)

Capriccio Italien, (top) with Afshin Mofid and Lisa Jackson; (bottom) with Maria Calegari and Joseph Duell (top: © Paul Kolnik; bottom: © Steven Caras)

Tchaikovsky Symphony No. 1, with Sean Lavery and Darci Kistler (© Paul Kolnik)

Rehearsing The Magic Flute at the School of American Ballet, (top) with Shawn Stevens;
(opposite, top) with Deidre Neal and Jock Soto; (bottom) with Stacey Calvert and Patricia Tomlinson (© Steven Caras)

The Magic Flute, opening night, the New York City Ballet, with Darci Kistler (© Martha Swope and overleaf)

The story has nothing to do with the plot of Mozart's opera except that both contain the enchanted instrument that made everyone dance. Balanchine had long ago acquired a piano score, and the full orchestral score was being sent, courtesy of the Tchaikovsky Foundation, from Russia via Germany. It was originally choreographed by Lev Ivanov and came with a ready-made libretto that gave me the sense of working with someone else's material. It was a chance to work with character, plot, mime and storytelling and with comedy. And it also gave me the chance to work with very young dancers.

What it set out were obstacles and problems, for I had not worked with any of these elements before. Since I was out to prove myself versatile as well as prolific, this was an excellent if terrifying opportunity. As a fillip, the director of the school extended the invitation further by asking if I would make a short curtain-raiser for the graduating division. Since I had been listening to Tchaikovsky, I recommended *Capriccio Italien*, a chestnut that Mr. Balanchine had made a wry face about when I had mentioned it for the Tchaikovsky festival.

So there I was committed to making two ballets at the same time, and with the real possibility that I'd have to start a third when the company break was over.

There would be three performances, and two casts of principals for *Flute*, but the final casting would be held off until two weeks before the performances. This would give me a chance to try a few of the kids in the roles to see which boy best suited which girl, and in fact, most of the other boys tried the boy's variation.

Capriccio had no alternate casts and since it is a short and straightforward piece of music it was fairly easy to set. I used two groups: one of tall boys and girls, big people, as I called them, and one of short people. The big people were in tights and tutus, very classical, and the little ones, led by a tiny Japanese whiz named Gen Horiuchi, were costumed in Italian peasant costumes from the company's production of *Bournonville Divertissements*. A few critics said this choice was autobiographical, the Bournonville

215

costumes and the way the small people danced referring to my Danish training and the classical part referring to Balanchine.

I certainly meant it to be a juxtaposition and I gambled that when Balanchine saw it he'd add it to the festival. He did and because of injuries and because other works weren't finished in time, it became the most frequently programmed piece in the festival. Its student cast couldn't believe how often they were appearing on the stage of the State Theater, and the audience began wondering when they'd stop seeing the work.

For all my dread, the making of *Flute* was total joy, and the kids were heartbreakingly willing to try anything. Their energy and enthusiasm, combined with a nervous shyness and a still raw edge to their dancing, made them splendid companions. A problem was that those who couldn't act could dance, those who were not such great dancers were natural actors, those boys who did the solos brilliantly were uninterested partners, and the good partners couldn't dance three steps. The trick was to do the best with what was available, and to promote and showcase them at their best.

Since they were all reluctant actors, I made them act big and exaggerated, my notions based more on silent comedy techniques than on actual mime, and the bigger, more outrageous they were, the better they were. The dancing was as sweet and adorable as could be and the mime as clownish, and I hoped one part would make the other easier.

In the final run-through, Mr. Balanchine offered numerous suggestions about the staging. It was a work that he had happy memories of, and one that he had long considered staging himself. He thought so well of my version that he decided it would be included in the company repertory the following season, with new costumes and a new orchestral score by Robert Irving (the one that finally arrived was incomplete, and the orchestra faked through a lot of it, not very convincingly).

As I thought would happen, before finishing *Magic Flute* and *Capriccio* I had to begin the work assigned me for the Tchaikovsky festival, the First Symphony, a work the composer called *Winter Dreams*. As it turned out, the other choreographers for the festival (Robbins, Taras, D'Amboise, Joseph

Duell, as well as Mr. Balanchine) had already started, and I had to fight for time and dancers in an overloaded schedule. I swiveled from rehearsing my ballets at the school to working on the First Symphony and also rehearsing my own performances, and dancing. Something had to suffer, and it was my physical condition. My back gave way, and I suffered painful muscle spasms.

After the premiere of *Histoire*, Mr. Balanchine told me to think about making my ballets a little simpler, not to make so many steps unless it was essential. The lesson seemed to me that I was cluttering the work by overchoreographing. With this new piece I intended to correct that. Perhaps Balanchine's caution fixed the design for what I would do in the symphony, for the music was so wanderingly structured and mysterious that I didn't want to match the vagueness but to cut through it, even oppose it, to discover its structural bones and impetus.

Because of a lack of time, I had to eliminate one movement, and as beautiful as it is, it was clear it would have to be the first. The second and fourth movements couldn't follow each other, and the other choice — that of dropping the second — was unthinkable, for it had the most danceable music. So the first was out. I decided there would be only one principal couple who would appear in all three movements but would have less and less to do in each. They would, in fact, disappear at the end, leaving the stage empty while the last pages of the score were played — this idea outraged many in the audience at the first performances.

The principals would not appear in the *scherzo*, and the fugue was set for eight couples, with the girls in tutus. By these decisions I was minimalizing the symphonic structure, concerning myself less with its parts, but with making these parts link together seamlessly, trying for a coherent flow and shape.

Tchaikovsky's music is suggestively programmatic, and ruthlessly I tried to avoid sentimental or story implications; rather, I wanted to work with the composer's image, "Winter Dreams." Vastness, sharp clear air. I wanted the work to tingle and to cause slight shivers. Thoughts of stillness, exhilaration, clarity, yet in a dream where everything vanishes finally, leaving only a hint (the entrance of the main couple is reversed in the exit — all comings and goings are blurred events).

I wanted to show the elegance of young Darci Kistler. She, partnered by Sean Lavery, was not meant to overwhelm the audience with pyrotechnics and spectacular technique. I deliberately held back both Darci and Sean, and held back the work, to try for mood and simplicity, for a kind of purity.

The piece opens with Darci and Sean entering from opposite sides, each making elliptical arcs till they meet upstage center. Intended as a chaste, calm, stately *pas de deux*, it is followed or interrupted by the entrance of the corps of six couples. The contrasting *scherzo* is for two couples, and here there is a release of technical vocabulary, but the setting is basically symmetrical (one dancer mirrors the choreography of the other) to hold the feel of simplicity. In the waltz that follows, the main couple reappears with the corps.

The orchestral fugue is matched by four battalions who interweave and change place in block formations for a feel of mass. Here I was hoping to correct a tendency I share with other young choreographers to match steps to the music, and now the combinations were always simpler than the music. The final exit is for the principal couple, who separate and exit to opposite sides, leaving an empty stage for the crescendos of the last bars.

During the finale I intended there to be an elaborate light show played on descending curtains formed of plastic tubes (these tubes were elements of the fixed set used for all performances during the Tchaikovsky festival), but these tubes flattened out light rather than bouncing it back, and the light rehearsals were stomach turning. We settled for a rather anemic play of blue and white lights.

The audience was confused by the vacant stage at the end, but I liked it just the way it was. It might be a horrible failure (it looks very beautiful to me), but rather than worry about correcting its faults, I was eager to start thinking about my next project.

Changes were suggested, especially for filling in the ending, or even making something happen during the ending. Some guessed that I had run out of rehearsal time and that later I'd finish the ballet.

For the Fall 1981 season, I did add a bit at the end to shorten the time the stage was empty; but I haven't yet made substantial changes in any of my works after their premieres, though this isn't something I have made a policy decision about. It's just that I haven't felt the urge yet. Mr. Balanchine makes one version in the shortest amount of time, and then over the years changes and reconsiderations creep in. He has added sections (in *Serenade* the *scherzo*), dropped sections (the birth of Apollo), and altered choreography. When he set *The Four Temperaments* for television, some thirty years after its premiere, he revised and "fixed" parts that he said he always wanted to fix but had never before had time to get around to.

Jerome Robbins has a different procedure. Before the opening night he makes three or four different versions, and practically as late as just before the curtain goes up he decides which will go. Once the curtain rises, that ballet is basically the ballet you will always see. He keeps it fixed, almost unalterably.

All my ballets have virtually the same cast they had on their openings (of course, the exceptions are when they have been set on other companies, or when a dancer is injured). I've made my ballets on specific dancers, and I know exactly who I want: principals, soloists, corps. And I don't see other dancers in these parts. Our ballet mistress, Rosemary Dunleavy, is constantly asking for me to cover the leads, but I like to refuse, preferring the risk of having the ballet dropped. Resetting, recasting, rethinking earlier works is still ahead for me.

As cliché as it may sound, I think that I am at my most honest when I choreograph. When I talk in public, I want my English to sound more impressive, more extensive than I think it is. When I am in front of an audience there are defensive mannerisms that creep into my personality, and I hide behind a performer's mask. But when I choreograph I search for what is really right, what is the best and clearest and most truthful. I avoid any big applause-getting moments unless they are required, I avoid imposing any extraneous effects, and I get furious when the dancers start acting up in my ballets.

This probably explains why I am so happy as a choreographer, for the time being. One of the greatest lessons my mother taught me as a little boy was that we don't know what will happen in the future. If we knew, it would ruin our lives, and not knowing is our greatest blessing. That's why I continue: to discover what will happen and where I'll be tomorrow.

Right now, choreography is the most important thing in my life professionally, but the one thing I hold above it is love. I would drop everything for it. The question comes down to one of priorities: as ambitious and professional as I am, I'd throw it all away for love. I don't think that a great virtue, but a weakness, and I've come to terms with it. To me, the loneliest life is the one without love.

I think of myself in contradictory ways. I consider myself tough, ambitious, level-headed. I don't waste time. I don't ponder over problems; I just go ahead and do whatever has to be done, and if I've made a mistake I'd rather take the consequences than have held off taking action. I am impulsive and spontaneous, and I'm moody and sentimental. The people I care about are never out of my mind, and one of my problems is that I tend to assume a lot of responsibility. It's as if by dealing with other people's problems, I set my own problems aside (perhaps a way of avoiding them without feeling guilty). I have some sense that I don't take good care of myself, but maybe that is a judgment I've inherited from my family, who've always been disapproving about the way I live, eat, and smoke. Another fault is impatience with people who are not close to me — with the people I love deeply I am unbelievably patient, and I'm very possessive.

There is so little time in the life of a dancer just to be, just to relax and do nothing or do something that has nothing whatsoever to do with dancing. It's when I don't dance I feel myself become alive in so many ways. It's then I see a different world, where there is time to focus on so many things that I enjoy: theater, decorating, architecture, movies, reading, music.

It isn't that I feel I've given anything up by being a dancer; it's just that I see how demanding a dancer's life must be, and what aspects of life you don't have time for.

I know that my attitudes have changed, that I have grown as I've changed (who knows, by the time these words are read I'll have changed my mind about what I'm saying here). For one thing, when I came to New York I came to a much more sophisticated world than I had known: it was more intense professionally, and more relaxed emotionally. I became more tolerant, and I became more focused. I also learned how to love and how to receive love. I feel that I've become liberated, and in my heart of hearts I feel I do what I want, that I do exactly what I like to do.

With that I've become more outspoken about what I think, more emphatic and opinionated. What keeps me from becoming unbearably pompous is that I am always willing to learn and I am always forcing my friends to tell me what I don't know. I am fiendish that way. For all my bluster, I am really very flexible, open to change. I'm probably thought inconsistent, but that's because I work so hard at leaving myself open.

The world is full of people who want you to act in what they perceive is the right way. They'd have you dance and choreograph and behave in the manner they think most appropriate (their way). They want you to write the books they want to read, etc., etc. I find that utterly boring. I don't want to be told how to act or dance, or what to say, or what I should choreograph for whom, or what I should think, or to be told when to shut up, or to be told not to do or say something because it might offend or embarrass. In fact, I am trying hard to be less "politically smart," and though I hope I'm diplomatic, I strive to be true to my feelings and thoughts.

I see that I've become outspoken about my profession, for now I feel some real urge that comes from my deepening commitment to dance, to see that standards are raised. I want to make dance a better functioning profession, both artistically and organizationally. I am sick and tired of this pathetic inadequacy I am seeing: I'd like the audience to be alert to fakery, I want inadequate and weak ballet masters axed if they can't cut it. I get furious when I read a good review of something anyone true to himself would recognize as garbage. Naturally, I'm not so lofty as to be above politics or diplomacy, and I understand the need for that if the arts are to survive financially and if the artists are to have the time to progress, but I see a lot of promotion of certain artists by critics that is what I call political — and the only other conclusion I can make is that the critic must have a lack of knowledge. Sometimes a critic overpraises, maybe out of a need to call attention to work that is worthy, but the effect on the dancer or choreographer and on artistic standards can be devastating. What is intended as a service becomes a disservice. The work has been overpraised, and the audience's expectations become so high that they can only be puzzled, and finally disappointed with dance as a whole, when they encounter the work — or worse, they ignore their own good sense and believe what they have been told. Then also, intense pressure has been placed on the artist to produce successes so that he can't develop and experiment and ever be allowed to fail. How can someone in his thirties be called a master, or one of the greatest whatever? — well, Mozart "and friends" excluded, of course.

Having made the decision to stay in the dance world for the whole of my life, I feel I have to examine every part of this world, but I can only protect that little part of it that's mine. So I am left with the feeling that there is the other dance world and mine, and that in my world I have to keep everything straight and clear and true. The easiest thing to do in the world is to commercialize ourselves, and satisfying that temptation would seem to make life so much easier: there would be more money, the public would be happy all the time and not made uneasy sometimes, if you were famous you'd get seated at fancy restaurants right away instead of having to wait with the real folks, you'd pal around with other famous people. But who becomes a dancer to make money? No one. Maybe there are five dancers in the world who make what I consider big bucks, but that's it.

Since this life seems so hard, so thoroughly involving, so relentless in its demands, it is hard to make others know what the rewards are. I've thought that maybe the reason people outside the profession are shy around dancers is because our motives must seem so pure, so untypical, so strange. The reward is dancing itself. It is the most satisfying thing for a dancer to do. There are no fringe benefits. Dancers don't need them.

Repertoire and Choreographed Works

*T*he following list, compiled with the invaluable assistance of Leslie Bailey, notes the ballets Peter Martins has performed principal roles in, and the ballets he has made. Those ballets starred are ballets first performed by Mr. Martins, and the partners starred appeared in the first performance also. The groupings are by company and occasions. In some few cases because of incomplete documentation we've made a guess at just when the works entered Mr. Martins' repertoire.

REPERTOIRE

Royal Danish Ballet

1964

Garden Party. Ch. Frank Schaufuss, mus. Alexander Glazunov. Partner: Anna Laerkesen.

*Moods. Ch. Hans Brenaa, mus. Franz Liszt. Partner: *Lise La Cour. Debut with Royal Danish Ballet in this work.

1965

Moon Reindeer. Ch. Birgit Cullberg, mus. Knudåge Riisager. Partners: Toni Lander, Anna Laerkesen. First performance of this role was on tour in San Diego, California.

Konservatoriet. Ch. August Bournonville, mus. Holger Simon Paulli.

Napoli, Act III. Ch. August Bournonville, mus. Holger Simon Paulli, Edvard Helsted, Hans Christian Lumbye.

The Kermesse at Bruges. Ch. August Bournonville, mus. Holger Simon Paulli. Production by Flemming Flindt.

Etudes. Ch. Harald Lander, mus. Knudåge Riisager, after Carl Czerny.

The Whims of Cupid and the Ballet Master. Ch. Vincenzo Galeotti, mus. Jens Lolle. Production by Hans Brenaa.

1966

*The Three Musketeers. Ch. Flemming Flindt, mus. Georges Delerue. Partners: *Kirsten Simone, *Anna Laerkesen. Premiere, May 11, 1966. Role: Portos.

Symphony in C. Ch. George Balanchine, mus. Georges Bizet.

The Nutcracker. Ch. Marius Petipa, mus. Peter Ilyich Tchaikovsky.

1967

The Miraculous Mandarin. Ch. Flemming Flindt, mus. Béla Bartók.

The Young Man Who Must Marry. Ch. Flemming Flindt, mus. Per Nørgaard. Libretto after
     Eugène Ionesco's play *Jacques ou la soumission.*

*Gala Variations. Ch. Flemming Flindt, mus. Knudåge Riisager. Partners: *Kirsten Simone,
     Anna Laerkesen.

Le Loup. Ch. Roland Petit, mus. Henri Dutilleux.

Apollo. Ch. George Balanchine, mus. Igor Stravinsky.

Swan Lake, Act II. Ch. Flemming Flindt, after Marius Petipa and Lev Ivanov. Partner:
     Kirsten Simone.

1968

Jeu de Cartes. Ch. John Cranko, mus. Igor Stravinsky.

Serenade. Ch. George Balanchine, mus. Peter Ilyich Tchaikovsky.

Graduation Ball. Ch. David Lichine, mus. Johann Strauss, arr. and orch. Antol Dorati.

Aimez-Vous Bach? Ch. Brian Macdonald, mus. Johann Sebastian Bach. Created role in RDB
     production.

1969

Bagage. Ch. Henryk Tomaszewski, mus. Giovanni Pergolesi.

*Aspects. Ch. Frank Schaufuss.

The Lady and the Fool. Ch. John Cranko, mus. Giuseppe Verdi, arr. Charles Mackerras.

Cicatricis. Ch. Eske Holm.

1976

La Sylphide, Ch. August Bournonville, mus. Hermann Løvenskjøld.

1979

A Folk Tale. Ch. August Bournonville, mus. Johann Peter Emilius Hartman and Niels
     Wilhelm Gade. Role: Junker Ove.

Danish Television: 1967–69

*Dream Pictures. Ch. Emilie Walbom, mus. Hans Christian Lumbye.

Helios. Ch. Elsa-Marianne von Rosen, mus. Carl Nielsen.

The Blade of Grass. Ch. Nini Theilade.

The Net. Ch. Rikki Septimus.

The Dream. Ch. Elsa-Marianne von Rosen.

New York City Ballet

1967

Apollo. Ch. George Balanchine, mus. Igor Stravinsky. Partners include: Suzanne Farrell, Kay Mazzo, Heather Watts, Allegra Kent. Debut role with NYCB as guest artist in Edinburgh, August 28, 1967.

The Nutcracker. Ch. George Balanchine, mus. Peter Ilyich Tchaikovsky. Partners include: Suzanne Farrell, Melissa Hayden, Mimi Paul, Allegra Kent, Kay Mazzo, Patricia McBride, Collen Neary, Merrill Ashley, Heather Watts, Violette Verdy, Darci Kistler. American debut with NYCB, December 25, 1967, as Cavalier.

1968

Diamonds, from full evening work, *Jewels.* Ch. George Balanchine, mus. Peter Ilyich Tchaikovsky. Partners include: Suzanne Farrell, Allegra Kent, Kay Mazzo, Merrill Ashley, Kyra Nichols.

Symphony in C. Ch. George Balanchine, mus. Georges Bizet. Partners include: Karin von Aroldingen, Melissa Hayden, Violette Verdy, Suzanne Farrell, Allegra Kent, Heather Watts, Darci Kistler. Roles: Danced both First and Second Movements.

Swan Lake. Ch. George Balanchine, after Ivanov, mus. Peter Ilyich Tchaikovsky. Partners include: Melissa Hayden, Allegra Kent, Kay Mazzo, Suzanne Farrell, Violette Verdy.

Liebeslieder Walzer. Ch. George Balanchine, mus. Johannes Brahms. Partners include: Suzanne Farrell, Karin von Aroldingen.

1969

Dances at a Gathering. Ch. Jerome Robbins, mus. Frederic Chopin. Partners include: Patricia McBride, Suzanne Farrell, Heather Watts, Kyra Nichols. Roles: Boy in Green, Boy in Brown.

Tchaikovsky Piano Concerto No. 2 (Ballet Imperial). Ch. George Balanchine, mus. Peter Ilyich Tchaikovsky. Partners include: Patricia McBride, Merrill Ashley, Suzanne Farrell, Heather Watts, Kyra Nichols. The title change from *Ballet Imperial* to *Piano Concerto No. 2* occurred in 1973 when this work was revived for Patricia McBride and PM.

1970

Serenade. Ch. George Balanchine, mus. Peter Ilyich Tchaikovsky. Partners include: Kay Mazzo, Suzanne Farrell, Allegra Kent.

In the Night. Ch. Jerome Robbins, mus. Frederic Chopin. Partners include: *Violette Verdy, Melissa Hayden, Allegra Kent, Suzanne Farrell, Merrill Ashley. First role choreographed on PM at NYCB; premiere, January 29, 1970.

Divertimento No. 15. Ch. George Balanchine, mus. W. A. Mozart. Partners include: Merrill Ashley, Melissa Hayden, Suzanne Farrell.

1971

Tchaikovsky Suite No. 3. Ch. George Balanchine, mus. Peter Ilyich Tchaikovsky. Partners include: Kay Mazzo, Patricia McBride, Merrill Ashley, Heather Watts, Kyra Nichols. Role: Fourth Movement: Theme and Variations.

A Midsummer Night's Dream. Ch. George Balanchine, mus. Felix Mendelssohn. Partners include: Suzanne Farrell, Kay Mazzo, Merrill Ashley, Allegra Kent, Heather Watts, Melissa Hayden. Roles: Cavalier and Divertissement.

Pas de Deux (Tchaikovsky). Ch. George Balanchine, mus. Peter Ilyich Tchaikovsky. Partners include: Suzanne Farrell, Patricia McBride, Violette Verdy, Melissa Hayden, Heather Watts, Merrill Ashley, Gelsey Kirkland.

The Goldberg Variations. Ch. Jerome Robbins, mus. Johann Sebastian Bach. Partner: *Karin von Aroldingen; also Brown Boy with Patricia McBride, Suzanne Farrell, Heather Watts. Roles: Premiere role, Purple Boy; also danced Brown Boy later. Premiere, May 27, 1971.

Brahms-Schoenberg Quartet. Ch. George Balanchine, mus. Johannes Brahms, orch. Arnold Schoenberg. Partners include: (First Movement) Violette Verdy, Linda Yourth, Kay Mazzo, Melissa Hayden; (Second Movement) Patricia McBride; (Fourth Movement) Karin von Aroldingen, Suzanne Farrell. Roles: First, Second, Fourth Movements.

1972

Chopiniana (Les Sylphides). Ch. Michael Fokine, staged by Alexandra Danilova for this production, mus. Frederic Chopin. Partner: Kay Mazzo. NYCB premiere, January 20, 1972.

Don Quixote. Ch. George Balanchine, mus. Nicolas Nabokov. Partner: *Karin von Aroldingen, Merrill Ashley. Role: *Pas Classique Espagnol, added in 1972 to original 1965 production.

Stravinsky Violin Concerto. Ch. George Balanchine, mus. Igor Stravinsky. Partners include: *Kay Mazzo, Lourdes Lopez. Premiere, June 18, 1972, opening night of NYCB Stravinsky Festival.

Firebird. Ch. George Balanchine, mus. Igor Stravinsky. Partner: Karin von Aroldingen. First performance by PM in this ballet June 18, 1972, opening night of the Stravinsky Festival, a revival of the 1970 production with slight changes.

*Symphony in E-Flat. Ch. John Clifford, mus. Igor Stravinsky. Partner: *Gelsey Kirkland. Premiere, June 20, 1972, NYCB Stravinsky Festival.

*Duo Concertant. Ch. George Balanchine, mus. Igor Stravinsky. Partners: *Kay Mazzo, Suzanne Farrell. Premiere, June 22, 1972, NYCB Stravinsky Festival.

*Choral Variations on Bach's "Von Himmel Hoch." Ch. George Balanchine, mus. Igor Stravinsky. Partner: *Karin von Aroldingen. Premiere, June 25, 1972, closing night at NYCB Stravinsky Festival, its only performance.

Scènes de Ballet. Ch. John Taras, mus. Igor Stravinsky. Partner: Merrill Ashley.

1973

La Source. Ch. George Balanchine, mus. Léo Delibes. Partners: Kay Mazzo, Merrill Ashley, Suzanne Farrell.

An Evening's Waltzes. Ch. Jerome Robbins, mus. Frederic Chopin. Partner: Gelsey Kirkland. Role: Third Waltz.

1974

Concerto Barocco. Ch. George Balanchine, mus. Johann Sebastian Bach. Partners include: Suzanne Farrell, Heather Watts, Allegra Kent, Gelsey Kirkland.

Bartók No. 3. Ch. John Clifford, mus. Béla Bartók. Partner: Sara Leland.

Agon. Ch. George Balanchine, mus. Igor Stravinsky. Partners include: Allegra Kent, Suzanne Farrell, Kay Mazzo, Heather Watts.

Who Cares? Ch. George Balanchine, mus. George Gershwin. Partners include: Kay Mazzo, Patricia McBride, Darci Kistler.

Cortège Hongrois. Ch. George Balanchine, mus. Alexander Glazunov. Partners include: Patricia McBride, Kay Mazzo, Suzanne Farrell, Merrill Ashley, Kyra Nichols.

Coppélia. Ch. George Balanchine and Alexandra Danilova, after Marius Petipa, with additional choreography by George Balanchine. Partners include: Patricia McBride, Stephanie Saland, Muriel Aasen.

Afternoon of a Faun. Ch. Jerome Robbins, mus. Claude Debussy. Partners include: Patricia McBride, Allegra Kent, Kay Mazzo, Suzanne Farrell, Heather Watts.

1975

Raymonda Variations. Ch. George Balanchine, mus. Alexander Glazunov. Partners include: Suzanne Farrell, Patricia McBride, Merrill Ashley.

*In G Major. Ch. Jerome Robbins, mus. Maurice Ravel. Partners: *Suzanne Farrell, Ghislaine Thesmar, Heather Watts. Premiere, May 15, 1975, Ravel Festival, as *Concerto in G.* PM also performed this, with Suzanne Farrell, with the Paris Opera Ballet Company.

*Daphnis and Chloe. Ch. John Taras, mus. Maurice Ravel. Partners: *Nina Fedorova, Suzanne Farrell. Premiere, May 22, 1975, Ravel Festival.

*Tzigane. Ch. George Balanchine, mus. Maurice Ravel. Partner: *Suzanne Farrell. Premiere, May 29, 1975, Ravel Festival.

Stars and Stripes. Ch. George Balanchine, mus. John Philip Sousa, orch. Hershy Kay. Partners include: Colleen Neary, Violette Verdy, Melissa Hayden, Suzanne Farrell, Merrill Ashley, Heather Watts. Role: El Capitan.

1976

Allegro Brillante. Ch. George Balanchine, mus. Peter Ilyich Tchaikovsky. Partners include: Suzanne Farrell, Patricia McBride, Merrill Ashley, Heather Watts.

Chaconne. Ch. George Balanchine, mus. Christoph Willibald von Gluck. Partner: Suzanne Farrell. This ballet was created for the Hamburg Opera in 1963, and mounted for the NYCB for Suzanne Farrell and PM. NYCB premiere, January 22, 1976.

*Union Jack. Ch. George Balanchine, mus. traditional British tunes, adapted by Hershy Kay. Partners: *Kay Mazzo, Muriel Aasen, Heather Watts. Roles: Menzies, Royal Navy. Premiere, May 13, 1976.

Other Dances. Ch. Jerome Robbins, mus. Frederic Chopin. Partner: Suzanne Farrell. This ballet was first made for Natalia Makarova and Mikhail Baryshnikov. Suzanne Farrell and PM appeared in the NYCB production. NYCB premiere, November 26, 1976.

1977

Bournonville Divertissements. Ch. August Bournonville, staged for this production by Stanley Williams, mus. various. Partnered Suzanne Farrell in NYCB premiere, in pas de deux from *Flower Festival in Genzano,* later Merrill Ashley. NYCB premiere, February 3, 1977. In the spring of 1980, PM danced, with Ib Andersen, "Jockey Dance" from *From Siberia to Moscow* (mus. C. C. Moller) for a few performances as a part of *Bournonville Divertissements.*

*Vienna Waltzes. Ch. George Balanchine, mus. various. Partners: *Kay Mazzo, Heather Watts, Karin von Aroldingen. Role: Gold and Silver Waltz (mus. Franz Lehar). Premiere, June 16, 1977.

1978

La Valse. Ch. George Balanchine, mus. Maurice Ravel. Partner: Kay Mazzo.

*A Sketch Book: "Verdi Variations." Ch. Jerome Robbins, mus. Giuseppe Verdi. Partner: **Kyra Nichols. This pas de deux became the "Spring" section of *The Four Seasons,* and was first danced in that work by Kyra Nichols and Daniel Duell. Premiere, June 8, 1978.

1979

The Four Seasons. Ch. Jerome Robbins, mus. Giuseppe Verdi. Partner: Suzanne Farrell. Role: Autumn. This role was created for Mikhail Baryshnikov, and PM danced a variation different from Baryshnikov's.

Fancy Free. Ch. Jerome Robbins, mus. Leonard Bernstein. Partner: Stephanie Saland. The three men's solos were performed at a gala performance by Mikhail Baryshnikov, Jean-Pierre Frohlich, and PM on May 8, 1979. The NYCB premiere of the full work, with Jean-Pierre Frohlich, Bart Cook, and PM was on January 24, 1980.

Orpheus. Ch. George Balanchine, mus. Igor Stravinsky. Partner: Karin von Aroldingen. PM's first performance was in July 1979 in Saratoga, New York.

Donizetti Variations, Ch. George Balanchine, mus. Gaetano Donizetti. Partner: Kay Mazzo.

1980

Sonatine. Ch. George Balanchine, mus. Maurice Ravel. Partner: Suzanne Farrell.

Le Bourgeois Gentilhomme. Ch. George Balanchine, mus. Richard Strauss. Partners: Suzanne Farrell, Allegra Kent. Role: Cleonte. The role of Cleonte was made by George Balanchine for Rudolph Nureyev for a New York City Opera production, which had a co-choreography credit to Jerome Robbins. In a slightly different form, the work entered the repertory of NYCB on May 22, 1980, with Suzanne Farrell and PM.

*Robert Schumann's "Davidsbündlertänze." Ch. George Balanchine, mus. Robert Schumann. Partner: *Heather Watts. Premiere, June 19, 1980.

Scotch Symphony. Ch. George Balanchine, mus. Felix Mendelssohn. Partner: Suzanne Farrell.

1982

Mozartiana. Ch. George Balanchine, mus., Peter Ilyich Tchaikovsky. Partner: Suzanne Farrell.

The Magic Flute. Ch. Peter Martins, mus. Riccardo Drigo. Partner: Darci Kistler. PM stepped in for the NYCB premiere, when both scheduled "Lukes," Helgi Tomasson and Ib Andersen, were injured. This was the first time PM performed his own choreography. First made for School of American Ballet. NYCB premiere, January 21, 1982.

Concert Performances

In addition to the ballets listed in the NYCB repertoire, PM danced the following works in concert appearances.

Concerto. Ch. Kenneth MacMillan, mus. Dimitri Shostakovich. Partners: Gelsey Kirkland, Cynthia Gregory.

It's a Grand Night for Dancing. Ch. John Clifford, mus. Richard Rodgers. Partner: Gelsey Kirkland. PM replaced Mr. Clifford for a NY Promenades Concert series.

Paquita. Ch. Marius Petipa, staged by Alexandra Danilova, mus. Leon Minkus. Partner: Lourdes Lopez.

*Gli Uccelli (The Birds). Ch. Robert Weiss, mus. Ottorino Respighi. Partner: *Kay Mazzo. Presented at Caramoor Music Festival, June 16, 1979.

Le Corsaire. Ch. Marius Petipa, mus. Leon Minkus. Partner: Heather Watts.

National Ballet of Canada

Giselle. Ch. Jules Perrot and Jean Corelli, mus. Adolphe Adam. Partners: Lynn Seymour, Natalia Makarova, in concert with Kay Mazzo.

Swan Lake. Ch. Erik Bruhn, mus. Peter Ilyich Tchaikovsky. Partners: Lynn Seymour, Natalia Makarova.

London Festival Ballet

Les Sylphides. Ch. Michael Fokine, mus. Frederic Chopin. Partner: Mimi Paul.

Swan Lake. Ch. Marius Petipa and Lev Ivanov, mus. Peter Ilyich Tchaikovsky. Partner: Maina Gielgud.

The Sleeping Beauty. Ch. Marius Petipa, mus. Peter Ilyich Tchaikovsky. Partners: Mimi Paul, Lynn Seymour, and in concerts with Violette Verdy and Cynthia Gregory.

Hartford Ballet

Romeo and Juliet. Ch. Michael Uthoff, mus. Serge Prokofiev. Partner: *Judith Gosnell.
Premiere, February 18, 1981.

National Ballet of Washington

The Sleeping Beauty. Ch. Marius Petipa, mus. Peter Ilyich Tchaikovsky. Partner: Violette
Verdy. Performance in Miami, Florida.

U.S. Television Appearances

"Three by Balanchine." *Duo Concertant,* with Kay Mazzo. *Serenade,* with Kay Mazzo. Filmed
in Berlin, Germany, in November 1973. First aired in United States, May 21, 1975.
PBS.

Dance in America series (PBS):

1. "Choreography by Balanchine: Part One," first aired December 14, 1977. *Tzigane,*
danced with Suzanne Farrell.
2. "Choreography by Balanchine: Part Two," first aired December 21, 1977. *Diamonds,*
danced with Suzanne Farrell. *Stravinsky Violin Concerto,* danced with Kay Mazzo.
3. "Choreography by Balanchine: Part Three," first aired November 29, 1978. *Chaconne,*
danced with Suzanne Farrell.
4. "Choreography by Balanchine: Part Four," first aired March 7, 1979. *Allegro Brillante,*
danced with Suzanne Farrell.
5. "Two Duets," first aired February 20, 1980. *Calcium Light Night,* choreographed by PM,
with Heather Watts and Ib Andersen.
6. "Bournonville Dances," first aired May 24, 1982. Pas de deux from *Flower Festival in
Genzano,* danced with Merrill Ashley.

Robert Schumann's "Davidsbündlertänze," first aired January 5, 1982. CBS Cable.

"A Dancer's Life." Danish TV documentary (1978), first aired in United States March
1982. CBS Cable.

Film

The Turning Point, dir. Herbert Ross. Twentieth Century Fox, released November 1977.
With Suzanne Farrell danced excerpt from *Tchaikovsky Pas de Deux.*

235

CHOREOGRAPHED WORKS
New York City Ballet Repertory

Calcium Light Night. Mus. Charles Ives. Set: Steven Rubin. Section premiered, January 7, 1977, Brooklyn College, Brooklyn, New York. Official world premiere, October 1977, Spokane, Washington, NYCB premiere, January 19, 1978, New York State Theater, Lincoln Center, New York. Cast: Heather Watts, Daniel Duell.

Tricolore: Pas de Basque section. Mus. Georges Auric. Sets and costumes: Rouben Ter-Arutunian. Premiere, May 18, 1978, New York State Theater, Lincoln Center, New York. Cast: Colleen Neary, Adam Lüders.

Rossini Pas de Deux. Mus. Gioacchino Rossini. Premiere, June 8, 1978, as part of *A Sketch Book,* New York State Theater, Lincoln Center, New York. Cast: Heather Watts, Sean Lavery.

Sonate di Scarlatti. Mus. Domenico Scarlatti. Costumes: Ben Benson. Premiere July 19, 1979, as *Giardino di Scarlatti,* Saratoga Performing Arts Center, Saratoga Springs, New York. New York premiere, November 13, 1979, New York State Theater, Lincoln Center, New York. Cast: Heather Watts, Bart Cook.

Eight Easy Pieces. Mus. Igor Stravinsky. Premiere, January 16, 1980, Alice Tully Hall, Lincoln Center, New York, Benefit Performance for Dance Collection of the New York Public Library. NYCB premiere, January 24, 1980, New York State Theater, Lincoln Center, New York. Cast: Susan Gluck, Roma Sosenko, Stacy Caddell.

Lille Suite. Mus. Carl Nielsen. Costumes: Ben Benson, after a concept by Otto Nielsen. Premiere, as *Tivoli,* August 23, 1980, Tivoli Concert Hall, Copenhagen, Denmark. American premiere, October 10, 1980, John F. Kennedy Center for the Performing Arts, Washington, D.C. New York premiere, November 11, 1980, New York State Theater, Lincoln Center, New York. Cast: Heather Watts, Ib Andersen. Ballet dedicated to Niels-Jørgen Kaiser.

Suite from Histoire du Soldat. Mus. Igor Stravinsky. Costumes: Ben Benson. Premiere, January 29, 1981, New York State Theater, Lincoln Center, New York. Cast Darci Kistler, Ib Andersen, Jean-Piere Frohlich, Kyra Nichols, Heather Watts, Victor Castelli, Bart Cook, Daniel Duell.

Capriccio Italien. Mus. Peter Ilyich Tchaikovsky. Premiere, School of American Ballet, Sixteenth Annual Workshop Performances, May 9 and May 11, 1981, Juilliard Theater, Lincoln Center, New York. Cast: Lisa Jackson, Afshin Mofid, Gen Horiuchi. NYCB Production: Opening production of the NYCB Tchaikovsky Festival, June 4, 1981, with The School of American Ballet Workshop. Cast: as above.

The Magic Flute. Mus. Riccardo Drigo. Premiere, School of American Ballet, Sixteenth Annual Workshop Performances, May 9 and May 11, 1981, Juilliard Theater, Lincoln Center, New York. Cast: 1. Shawn Stevens, Sean Savoye, 2. Katrina Killian, Jock Soto. NYCB Production: sets: David Mitchell, costumes: Ben Benson. Premiere, January 21, 1982, New York State Theater, Lincoln Center, New York. Opening night cast: Darci Kistler, Peter Martins.

Symphony No. 1. Mus. Peter Ilyich Tchaikovsky. Costumes: Ben Benson. Premiere, June 6, 1981, NYCB Tchaikovsky Festival production. Cast: Darci Kistler, Sean Lavery, Lisa Hess, Lourdes Lopez, Afshin Mofid, Kipling Houston.

Piano-Rag-Music. Mus. Igor Stravinsky. Costumes: Ben Benson. Premiere, June 10, 1982, NYCB Stravinsky Centennial Celebration, New York State Theater, New York. Cast: Darci Kistler, Cornel Crabtree, Afshin Mofid, Peter Schetter, Ulrik Trojaborg.

Concerto for Two Solo Pianos. Mus. Igor Stravinsky. Premiere, June 13, 1982, NYCB Stravinsky Centennial Celebration, New York State Theater, Lincoln Center, New York. Cast: Heather Watts, Ib Andersen, Jock Soto.

Companies Other Than NYCB

Tango-Tango. Mus. Jacob Gade, Igor Stravinsky. For John Curry's "Ice Dancing." Premiere, December 1978, Felt Forum, New York. Cast: Jo Jo Starbuck, John Curry.

Dido and Aeneas, Mus. Henry Purcell. Stage dir. Frank Corsaro, pantomime scenes directed in collaboration with George Balanchine. Premiere, April 8, 1979, New York City Opera production, New York State Theater, Lincoln Center, New York.

Sonate di Scarlatti. Mus. Domenico Scarlatti. Het Nationale Ballet (Dutch National Ballet), Amsterdam, The Netherlands. Production April 1981.

Delibes Divertissement. Mus. Léo Delibes. Sets: David Mitchell. Premiere, School of American Ballet, Seventeenth Annual Workshop Performances, May 1 and May 3, 1982. Cast: Shawn Stevens, Carlo Merlo.

AWARDS

1977: Dance Magazine Award. Cue Magazine Golden Apple Award
1978: Nijinsky Prize
1980: Danish-American Society: Man of the Year
1981: New York City Award of Honor for Arts and Culture
     Associate Fellow, Calhoun College, Yale University

Overleaf: Photograph © Michael Avedon

INDEX

(Numbers in ITALICS *refer to illustrations.)*